PRINCETON REVIEW

human brain
coloring
workbook

PRINCETON REVIEW

human brain
coloring
workbook

by **Kapil Gupta**, M.D.

Illustrated by **Kristen Wienandt** and
Sally Cummings

Random House, Inc.
New York 1999
http://www.randomhouse.com

Princeton Review Publishing, L.L.C.
2315 Broadway
New York, NY 10024
E-mail: info@review.com

ISBN: 0-679-77885-3

Editor: Rachel Warren
Designer: Kirsten Ulve
Production Editor: James Petrozzello
Production Supervisor: Chee Pae
Manufactured in the United States of America on partially recycled paper

9 8 7 6 5 4 3

For Aradhana, Mom, and Dad

In Appreciation of...

Evan Schnittman, Editor-In-Chief: We've planned a book for so long, and finally, here we are. Thanks for your guidance and friendship.

Rachel Warren, Editor: It's wonderful to work with an editor as kind and cooperative as you. Thanks for making this a smooth ride.

Kristin Wienandt and Sally Cummings, Artists: Without you, this would only be half a book. Your talent is undeniable, as is your professionalism. We didn't converse much, but we didn't have to; the quality of your work said it all.

Kirstin Ulve, Adam Hurwitz, Evelin Sanchez-O'Hara, Robert McCormack, and Matthew Reilly: Your work on the layout, design and production is quite impressive. Well done.

Aradhana, My Wife: You are always the most important person, in this and every endeavor.

Preface

The brain is the most fascinating and most important of all biological systems.

Studying its anatomy is a formidable task, especially since much of it remains unknown. Nevertheless, I have done my best to prepare a text that will guide you through the anatomical mazes inherent in this wondrous system.

The major structures and systems of the brain and spinal cord are discussed in text and diagram format. Each plate of diagrams is accompanied by text that explains the anatomy of that particular structure or system. Throughout the text are a number of coloring instructions to help you properly organize the material. Remember that coloring is a method of active learning that facilitates understanding and recall.

A knowledge of anatomy unsupported by physiology is of a waste of time. What good is it to know where structures are located if you don't know what they do? Often, the reason that many structures are located where they are is because their physiology requires them to be there. For this reason I have included discussions of physiology, where relevant, in order to provide you with a contextual understanding of the material.

Some of you may be striving for a career in clinical medicine or other healthcare professions, and others may plan for a career in research and teaching. Either way, a knowledge of anatomy and physiology is essential in the clinical arena. The knowledge of neuroanatomy and neurophysiology is important because it can be applied to a further understanding of human function and human disease. As a result, I have included clinical correlates to help you apply your knowledge to clinical medicine.

The end of the book contains a cross-sectional atlas of both the human brain and spinal cord. This will help you summarize the locations of different structures at different depths of the brain.

I trust you will enjoy your study of the human brain, and I hope this book will enable you to do so.

Kapil Gupta, M.D.

Table of Contents

the developing central nervous system

Chapter 1-1: The Neural Tube

In discussing neurodevelopment, we will begin on the 18th day of development as this day marks the formation of the **neural tube (A)**. It is from the neural tube that the entire central nervous system (CNS; the brain and spinal cord) develops. The three main layers of the human embryo, at this point, from outermost to innermost are the ectoderm, mesoderm (not shown), and the endoderm. The CNS is derived from the midline portion of the **ectoderm (B)**, which is known as the **neural plate (C)**.

[Color A, B, and C different colors, blending between B and C; color C a darker color than B.]

Cells within the neural plate proliferate, forming an indentation called the **neural groove (D)**, which closes to form the neural tube, with its hollow **central canal (F)**. The initial point of closure of the neural tube is important because it marks the location of the neck; from this point the neural tube continues to close cephalad (toward the head), and caudad (away from the head).

[You may want to color F black.]

As could be expected, the rostral and intermediate portions, respectively, develop into the cerebral hemishpheres and brainstem, the caudal portion develops into the spinal cord, and the brain ventricles develop from the neural tube cavity. When the neural plate invaginates to form the neural groove, cells of the lateral margin of the neural plate remain isolated from the neural tube and lie between it and the ectoderm. This group of cells becomes the **neural crest (E)**; the neural crest gives rise to the dorsal root ganglion, sensory ganglia of the cranial nerves, autonomic ganglia, adrenal medulla, and melanocytes. The fusion of all parts of the neural tube is complete by day 28.

Clinical Correlates: *If the neural tube fails to close, a variety of diseases result; they are collectively referred to as neural tube defects. One example of this is a myelocele, a condition in which the neural tube fails to close and a part of the spinal cord protrudes through the spine at the area of this malclosure. When the neural tube fails to close, or if it reopens, caudally the result is an outpouching of the spinal cord through an unclosed area of the spinal column, a condition known as myelomeningocele. When the neural tube fails to close at its cephalic end, the result is an absence of the brain and calvarium, a condition known as anencephaly. The exact cause of neural tube defects is unknown.*

●● Neural tube	A	● Neural plate	C	● Neural crest	E
○ Ectoderm	B	○ Neural groove	D	● Central canal	F

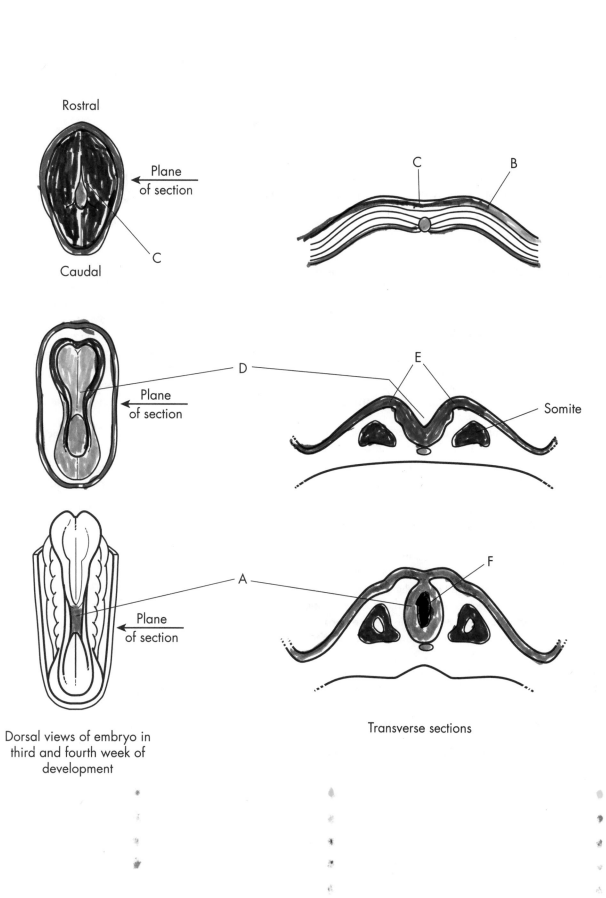

Rostral

Caudal

Plane
of section

C

C

B

Plane
of section

D

E

Somite

Plane
of section

A

F

Dorsal views of embryo in
third and fourth week of
development

Transverse sections

Chapter 1-2: Overview of the Brain and Ventricles

Once the neural tube has closed, three cavities form at its cephalic end; the **forebrain (A)**, **midbrain (B)**, and **hindbrain (C)**.

[Color A, B, and C different colors, and set aside these colors.]

These cavities are also known as the prosencephalon, mesencephalon, and rhombencephalon, respectively. This stage of their development is commonly referred to as the *3-vesicle stage*. At this stage, 2 flexures (bending points) are evident; **the cephalic flexure (D)** and the **cervical flexure (E)**; the cephalic flexure lies in the area of the midbrain, and the cervical flexure lies between the hindbrain and spinal cord. Over time, the forebrain and hindbrain divide further into two more vesicles. The forebrain divides into the **telencephalon (F)** and **diencephalon (G)**.

[Color F and G different shades of the color that you used to color A.]

The hindbrain divides into the **metencephalon (H)** and **myelencephalon (I)**.

[Color H and I different shades of the color you used to color C.]

The telencephalon eventually forms the cerebral hemispheres, the diencephalon develops into the thalamic system, the metencephalon gives rise to the pons and cerebellum, and the myelencephon gives rise to the medulla oblongata. This is known as the 5-vesicle stage, and during this stage a third flexure becomes prominent in the metencephalon, it is known as the **pontine flexure (J)**.

You may recall that the ventricular system of the brain develops from the inner cavity of the neural tube. Each of the cavities of the above structures develops into a part of the ventricular system: the cavity that develops into the cerebral hemisphere is the **lateral ventricle (K)**, and the cavities that develop into the diencephalon, midbrain, and hindbrain are the **third ventricle (L)**, **cerebral aqueduct (M)**, and the **fourth ventricle (N)**, respectively.

[Color K-N different shades of one color to demarcate one ventricular chamber from the next.]

The caudal cavity turns into the central canal of the spinal cord, and the third ventricle buds off to form the lateral ventricles. The ventricular system contains cerebrospinal fluid (CSF, not shown) which cushions the brain and circulates throughout the brain and spinal cord within the subarachnoid space (this will be discussed later). The majority of the CSF is manufactured by networks of blood vessels called the choroid plexus that lie within the lateral, third, and fourth ventricles. The choroid plexus is formed by the union of highly vascular mesoderm with the ependymal lining of the neural tube.

The caudal end of the neural tube becomes the spinal cord. Thus, by the sixth week the six major divisions of the central nervous system are evident: the telencephalon, diencephalon, mesencephalon, metencephalon, myelencephalon, and spinal cord.

Clinical Correlates: *If the cerebral aquedeuct becomes blocked (by tumor or for any other reason), the CSF will continue to back up like a log jam due to (1) the blockade, and (2) its continuous secretion from the choroid plexus. As a result, the ventricles would fill up with an excess of CSF, which would significantly raise the pressure within the cranial vault, creating a number of problems. This condition is termed hydrocephalus. There are two main types of hydrocephalus: communicating hydrocephalus and noncommunicating hydrocephalus. Communicating hydrocephalus is a condition in which the CSF flows freely from the ventricles into the subarachnoid space, where it builds up, creating dangerous pressure. In noncommunicating hydrocephalus, CSF flow from the ventricles is blocked, so that CSF never reaches the subarachnoid space; the example we cited earlier, therefore, is one of noncommunicating hydrocephalus, because CSF is prevented from leaving the ventricular system.*

○ Forebrain (Prosencephalon)	A	◐ Telencephalon	F	● Lateral ventricle	K
● Midbrain (Mesencephalon)	B	○ Diencephalon	G	◐ Third ventricle	L
◐ Hindbrain (Rhombencephalon)	C	● Metencephalon	H	◑ Cerebral aqueduct	M
○ Cephalic flexure	D	◐ Myelencephalon	I	◐ Fourth ventricle	N
○ Cervical flexure	E	● Pontine flexure	J		

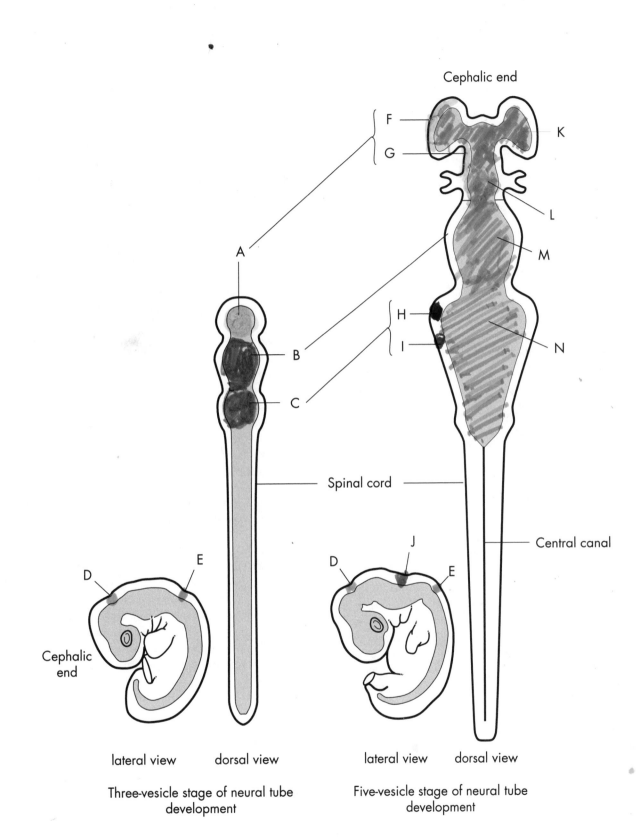

Cephalic end

F

G

K

A

B

L

C

M

H

I

N

Spinal cord

Central canal

D

E

Cephalic
end

D

J

E

lateral view   dorsal view

lateral view   dorsal view

Three-vesicle stage of neural tube
development

Five-vesicle stage of neural tube
development

Chapter 1-3: The Brain: Telencephalon and Cerebral Hemispheres

The prosencephalon (also known as the forebrain) divides into the **telencephalon (B)** and **diencephalon (G)** by the thirty-sixth day of embryonic development. At this time, a pair of lateral extensions known as the **optic vesicles (A)** have formed; one on each side of the prosencephalon, these will develop into the retina and their stalks will give rise to the two optic nerves.

[Color A a lighter shade of the color that you used for G.]

The pair of diverticula (pouches); one on each side of the prosencephalon, are the **telencephalon (B)**; their walls will become the cerebral hemispheres, and their cavities will become the **lateral ventricles (C)**. The lateral ventricles communicate with the **third ventricle (D)** via the **interventricular foramen (E)**.

[Color B the same color as in the previous diagram. Color E a lighter shade of the color you used to color C. Color D a different shade than C.]

The anterior boundary of the prosencephalon, third ventricle, and neural tube is marked by the **lamina terminalis (F)**. The optic vesicles, technically a part of the diencephalon, mark the boundary between the rostral (towards the head) and the caudal **diencephalon (G)**.

[Color G the same color as in the previous diagram.]

In the fifth week, the walls of the telencephalon begin to develop into the cerebral hemispheres, growing anteriorly, posteriorly, and dorsally (forward, backward, and upward), and eventually overlying the caudal diencephalon and posterior midbrain, assuming an oval configuration. The expansion continues anteriorly to produce the frontal poles, laterally and superiorly to

produce the parietal poles, posteriorly to produce the occipital poles, and inferiorly to produce the temporal poles. Also in the fifth week, a groove develops in the floor of each ventricle, these grooves deepen and grow with the developing hemispheres to become the **olfactory bulb (H)**.

The mesenchyme, which is a group of cells that make up the mesoderm, is located between the hemispheres and develops into the **falx cerebri (I)**. Vascular (blood vessel) mesenchyme joins the ependymal lining of the medial surface of the cerebral hemispheres, and the **choroid plexus (J)** is born. The cells of the forebrain vesicle, which were discussed earlier, are the origins of the basal ganglia and the hippocampus. A thickening of the walls of the forebrain vesicle produces the **hippocampus (K)**; the cells lining the floor of the forebrain form the corpus striatum, which separates into the **caudate nucleus (L)** and the **lentiform nucleus (M)**; the lentiform nucleus is made up of the **putamen (N)** and the **globus pallidus (O)**. The head of the caudate nucleus develops into three parts at the floor of the lateral ventricle; these parts then merge to form the caudate's tail and the amygdaloid complex.

[Color L, N, and O different shades of the same color. Use these same shades to color in the two parts of M.]

Eventually the smooth surface of the cerebral hemispheres develops into the cerebral cortex, producing convolutions and giving rise to gyri and sulci. Gyri may be seen as the mounds and sulci as the valleys in the drawing of the brain at six months. Appearing by the third month is the first sulcus, the **lateral sulcus (P)**. The floor of the sulcus develops into a small area known as the **(Q)** which eventually becomes covered by the ipsilateral (same side) cerebral hemisphere. Other sulci develop closer to the ninth month, which is the time of birth.

Optic vesicles	A	Diencephalon	G	Lentiform nucleus	M
Telencephalon	B	Olfactory bulb	H	Putamen	N
Lateral ventricles	C	Falx cerebri	I	Globus pallidus	O
Third ventricle	D	Choroid plexus	J	Lateral sulcus	P
Interventricular foramen	E	Hippocampus	K	Insula	Q
Lamina terminalis	F	Caudate nucleus	L		

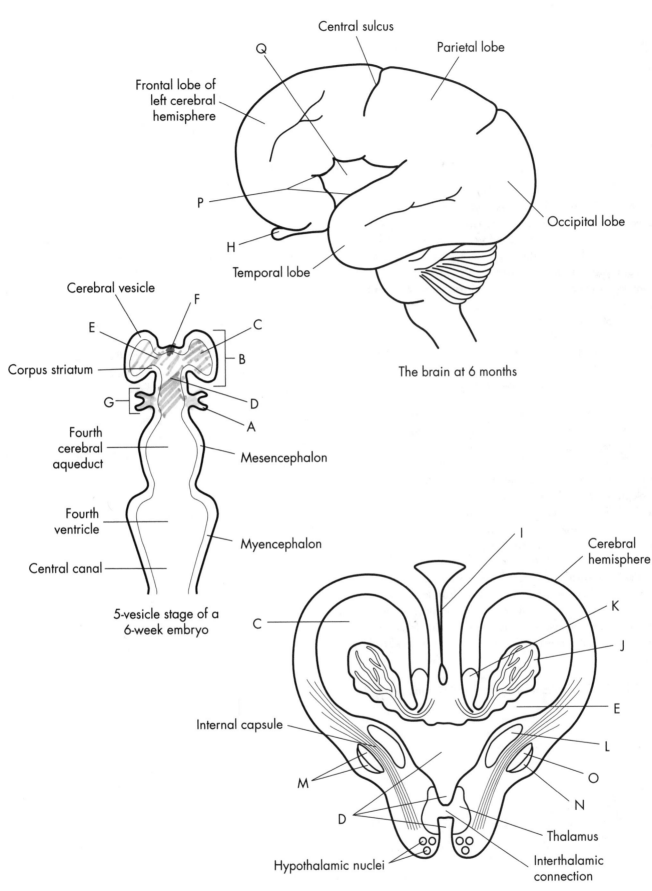

Central sulcus

Q

Parietal lobe

Frontal lobe of
left cerebral
hemisphere

P

H

Temporal lobe

Occipital lobe

The brain at 6 months

Cerebral vesicle

F

E

C

B

Corpus striatum

G

D

A

Fourth
cerebral
aqueduct

Mesencephalon

Fourth
ventricle

Myencephalon

Central canal

5-vesicle stage of a
6-week embryo

I

Cerebral
hemisphere

K

J

C

E

L

Internal capsule

O

N

M

D

Thalamus

Hypothalamic nuclei

Interthalamic
connection

Coronal section through cerebral hemispheres

Chapter 1-4: The Brain: Diencephalon and Mesencephalon

As we stated earlier, the diencephalon arises from the caudal segment of the forebrain vesicle. The cavity of the forebrain is the basis for development of the **third ventricle (A)**, and the rostral portions of the forebrain's roof invaginate to form the **choroid plexus of the third ventricle (B)**. The cephalic boundary of the diencephalon is the **interventricular foramen (C)**, and the caudal boundary is the posterior commissure, which is not shown.

[Color A the same color as was previously used for it, and color B a lighter shade of that color. Color C the same color as was previously used.]

The **hypothalamic sulcus (D)** marks the boundary between the thalamus and the hypothalamus; it is formed by longitudinal depressions that form on the alar plates of the forebrain. Thickening of the alar plate, in the lateral wall of the third ventricle, gives rise to the **thalamus (E)** on either side. During development the thalami grow closer to each other, narrowing the third ventricle, and fusing with each other to form the interthalamic adhesion, which is also known as the massa intermedia (not shown). Rapid cellular growth within the thalamus gives rise to the thalamic nuclear groups.

The **hypothalamus (F)** is formed by the portion of the alar plate that is inferior to the hypothalamic sulcus. In the hypothalamus, cells differentiate into the nuclear groups that are involved with endocrine and regulatory functions. A diverticulum arising from the floor of the diencephalon gives rise to the **infundibulum (G)**.

[Color F a lighter shade of the color that was used for E.]

The mesencephalon (midbrain), arises from the midbrain vesicle and forms the smallest portion of the brainstem. The cavity of this vesicle becomes drastically reduced and forms what is called the **cerebral aqueduct (H)**. The roof plate and the alar plates give rise to the **tectum (I)**, which will later consist of the superior and inferior colliculi. The growth of both alar plates results in two protuberances separated by a midline groove, and these protuberances will develop into the quadrigeminal plate (not shown). Then another depression appears that separates each protuberance into a **superior colliculus (J)** and an inferior colliculus (not shown), located on the posterior aspect of the midbrain. The neurocytes of the basal plate develop into the **nuclei of the third cranial nerve (K)** and fourth cranial nerve. The marginal layer of the basal plate forms the **basis pedunculi (L)**. The **red nucleus (M)** is believed to arise from the alar plate, and the origins of the **substantia nigra (N)** remain unclear.

[Use different colors for H-N. You may want to color M red, to help you remember its name.]

○	Third ventricle	A	○	Thalamus	E	○	Superior colliculus	J
○	Choroid plexus of the third ventricle	B	○	Hypothalamus	F	○	Nuclei of the third cranial nerve	K
○	Interventricular foramen	C	○	Infundibulum	G	○	Basis pedunculi	L
○	Hypothalamic sulcus	D	○	Cerebral aqueduct	H	○	Red nucleus	M
			○	Tectum	I	○	Substantia nigra	N

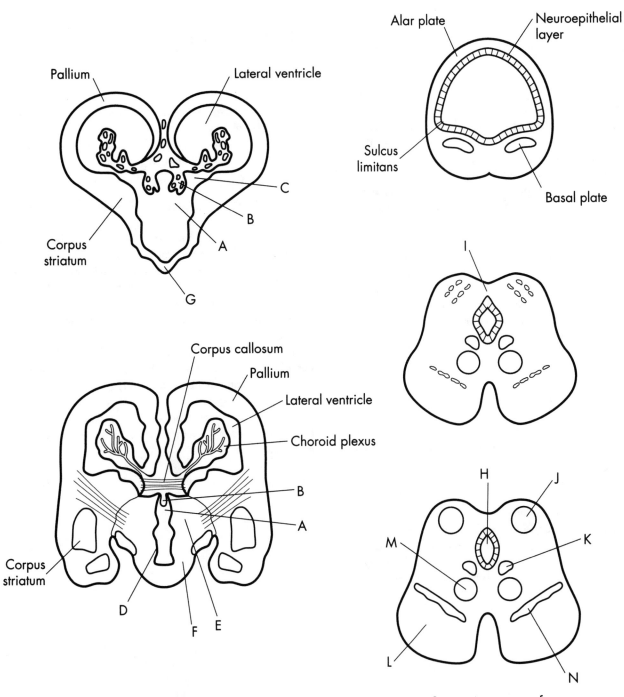

Pallium

Lateral ventricle

C

B

A

Corpus
striatum

G

Alar plate

Neuroepithelial
layer

Sulcus
limitans

Basal plate

I

Corpus callosum

Pallium

Lateral ventricle

Choroid plexus

B

A

Corpus
striatum

D

F   E

H   J

M   K

L   N

Coronal sections through
the diencephalon

Successive stages of
maturation of the
mesencephalon

Chapter 1-5: The Brain: Myelencephalon and Metencephalon

The myelencephalon arises from the hindbrain vesicle and then gives rise to the medulla oblongata, which is the caudal-most portion of the brain. Due to expansion of the **fourth ventricle (A)**, the lateral walls of the hindbrain vesicle move laterally at higher levels than they would otherwise. Therefore, the **alar plate (B)** ends up lying lateral to the **basal plate (C)**, and the **sulcus limitans (D)** separates them. Located on the floor of the fourth ventricle, the neurons of the basal plate differentiate into the motor nerve nuclei of cranial nerves IX, X, XI, and XII. The nerves of the alar plate develop into the sensory nerve nuclei of cranial nerves V, VIII, IX, and X, as well as three other nuclei; the gracile nucleus, cuneate nucleus, and **olivary nucleus (E)**. The **roof plate (J)** is composed of a single layer of ependymal cells underneath a sheet of pia mater; together these form the tela choroidea, which has projections that stretch into the fourth ventricle to form the **choroid plexus (F)**.

[Color B, C, D, and E different colors. Color F a lighter shade of the color used for A.]

Between the fourth and fifth months of fetal development, two openings (or foramen) in the roof plate develop to allow communication between the fourth ventricle and the subarachnoid space. One of these foramina develops as a pair; this pair of foramina is known as the foramen of Luschka. The other foramen that appears is called the foramen of Magendie; it will be shown and discussed in the chapter on the ventricular system.

The metencephalon gives rise to **pons (G)** and the cerebellum. The pons arises from the ventral aspect of the metencephalon, and the cerebellum arises from the dorsal aspect of the metencephalon. The dorsal portion of the pons, which is called the tegmentum, arises from the basal plate and lies in the floor of the fourth ventricle. Also arising from the basal plate are the motor nuclei of cranial nerves V, VI, and VII. The **pontine nuclei (H)** arise from the alar plate, as do the sensory nuclei of cranial nerves V and VII, and the vestibular and cochlear nuclei of cranial nerve VIII.

[Color H a lighter shade of the color used for G.]

The cerebellum is formed by the joining of the **rhombic lips (I)**, which bud off from the alar plates, and extend posteriorly over the **roof plate (J)**; the lips join in the midline and their fusion forms the part of the cerebellum known as the **vermis (K)**. The remaining pair of lateral regions give rise to the **cerebellar hemispheres (L)**. The dumbbell-shaped appearance of the cerebellum becomes evident by the third month; by the end of the fourth month, fissures begin to form, the first of which is the posterior fissure (not shown). The posterior fissure marks two anatomically significant boundaries: (1) it separates the caudal-most aspect of the cerebellum, harboring the **flocculus (M)** from its more rostral segments, and (2) it separates the **nodulus (N)** from the rest of the vermis. Neuroblasts give rise to the deep cerebellar nuclei.

[Color K, L, M, and N similar colors or different shades of one color.]

○ Fourth ventricle	A	○ Choroid plexus	F	○ Vermis	K
○ Alar plate	B	○ Pons	G	○ Cerebellar hemispheres	L
○ Basal plate	C	○ Pontine nuclei	H	○ Flocculus	M
○ Sulcus limitans	D	○ Rhombic lips	I	○ Nodulus	N
○ Olivary nucleus	E	○ Roof plate	J		

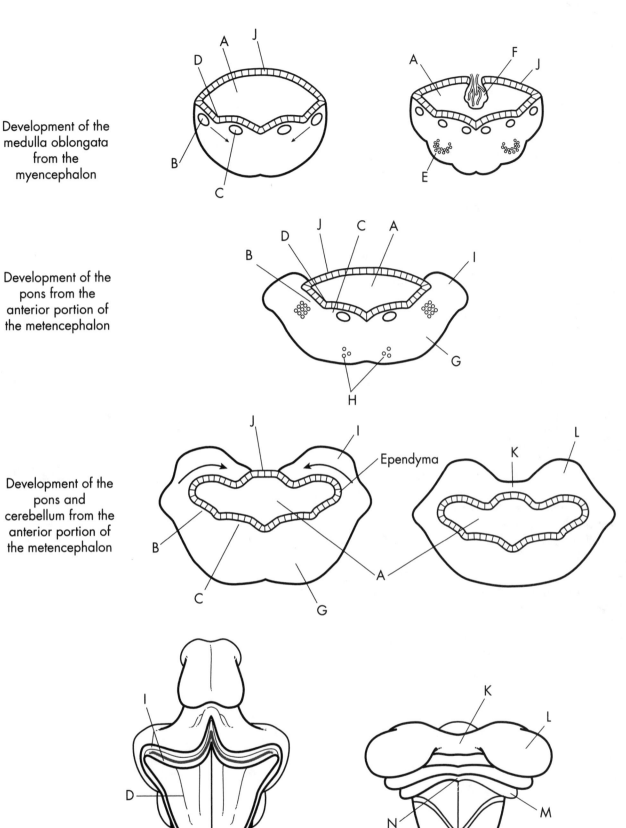

Development of the medulla oblongata from the myencephalon

Development of the pons from the anterior portion of the metencephalon

Development of the pons and cerebellum from the anterior portion of the metencephalon

Ependyma

Cerebellum, posterior, of 6-week embryo

Cerebellum, posterior, of 4-moth fetus

Chapter 1-6: The Spinal Cord

While the neural tube is being formed, a depression develops on each side of its lumen, or central cavity, that separates it into dorsal and ventral sections. This longitudinal depression is called the **sulcus limitans (C)**. The dorsal section is termed the **alar plate (A)** and the ventral section is termed the **basal plate (B)**.

[Color A and B different colors.]

The alar plate is involved with sensory function, and its neurons give rise to the spinal cord's **dorsal horn (D)**. The basal plate is not involved with the creation of brain regions that lie anterior to the midbrain; it is involved with motor conduction and its neurons occupy the spinal cord's **ventral horn (E)**.

[Color D and E different shades of the same color.]

Other neurons of the basal plate develop into interneurons, which are unique in that their axons are confined to the spinal cord. The **mantle layer (F)**, formed by neuroblasts that originate in the walls of the neural tube, gives rise to the **gray matter (G)** of the spinal cord. The **marginal layer (H)**, which is also formed from developing neuroblasts, contains ascending and descending axons, which are later myelinated, forming the **white matter (I)** of the spinal cord. After the third month, the cartilage and bones grow more rapidly than the spinal cord, and the spinal cord, which initially spanned the entire vertebral column, now ends up at the third lumbar vertebra. The caudal-most portion of the spinal cord is known as the conus medullaris, and from this extends a fiber known as the filum terminale.

[It may help you remember the structures if you color I a light color and G a dark color.]

The spinal cord extends from the foramen magnum on the posterior aspect of the skull, to the lower border of the first lumbar vertebra (L-1). It lies within the spinal column, whose 33 vertebra are divided into the following sections: 7 cervical, 12 thoracic, 5 lumbar, 4 sacral, and 4 coccygeal. **Mixed spinal nerves (J)** are formed from the union of **dorsal nerve roots (K)** and **ventral nerve roots (L)**. There are 31 pairs of spinal nerves and they divide the spinal cord into 5 segments: 8 cervical, 12 thoracic, 5 lumbar, 5 sacral, and 1 coccygeal. The coverings of the spinal cord are the same as those of the brain, from innermost to outermost: **pia mater (M)**, **arachnoid (N)**, and **dura mater (O)**.

[Use different shades of the same color for M-O: Make M the lightest, N darker, and O the darkest.]

○ Alar plate	A	○ Mantle layer	F	○ Dorsal nerve roots	K
○ Basal plate	B	○ Gray matter	G	○ Ventral nerve roots	L
○ Sulcus limitans	C	○ Marginal layer	H	○ Pia mater	M
○ Dorsal horn	D	○ White matter	I	○ Arachnoid	N
○ Ventral horn	E	○ Mixed spinal nerves	J	○ Dura mater	O

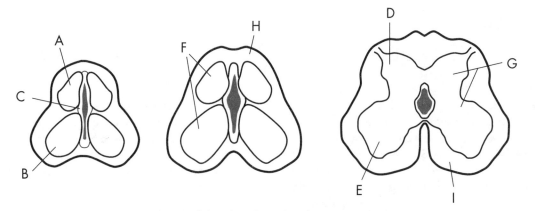

Transverse sections of the spinal cord with progressive maturation

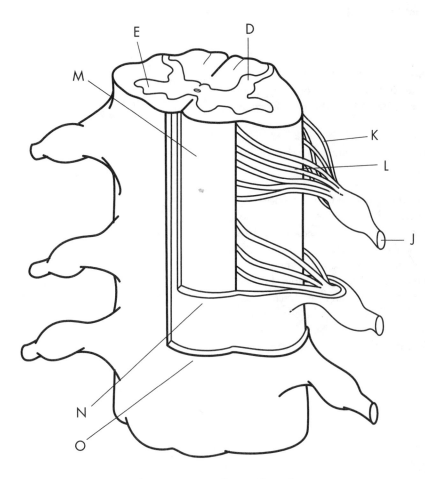

Anterior view of spinal cord

Chapter 1-7: Neurons and Glia

There are two principal cellular components of the nervous system: neurons and glia. The neural plate, and early on, the neural tube contain a layer of pluripotent epithelial stem cells that go on to form the cells of the CNS, with the exception of the microglia. The epithelial stem cells then divide to form fusiform neuroblasts and spindle-shaped glioblasts. Fusiform neuroblasts are formed first and make up the mantle layer of the neural tube, developing into **bipolar neuroblasts (A)**. One of the cytoplasmic processes of the cell stretches to form the axon and the other develops a complex dendritic network. It is now considered a **multipolar neur-oblast (B)**, and will develop into a nerve.

[Color A and B different shades of the same color.]

Glioblasts may develop into astrocytes, **oligodendrocytes (C)**, or **ependymal cells (D)**. There are 2 types of astrocytes: **protoplasmic astrocytes (E)** and **fibrous astrocytes (F)**.

[Color C and D different colors; color E and F different shades of the same color.]

Protoplasmic astrocytes predominate in the gray matter and fibrous astrocytes predominate in the white matter; no functional difference is known between the two types. Astrocytes act as phagocytes and form scars in the brain in response to injury. In addition, their foot processes abut cerebral capillaries and, therefore, aid in the development of the blood-brain barrier. Oligodendrocytes are responsible for forming the myelin sheath around axons in the CNS. The counterpart of the oligodendrocyte is the Schwann cell, which myelinates axons of the peripheral nervous system (PNS). One difference between the myelina-

tors is that an oligodendrocyte can envelope more than one axon, whereas a Schwann cell can only myelinate one axon. As you may recall, the myelin sheath serves to accelerate signal conduction along axons. Ependymal cells line the ventricular system and act as a barrier between the ventricular fluid and the brain parenchyma.

Clinical Correlates: *As was previously discussed, Schwann cells and oligodendrocytes myelinate axons of the PNS and CNS, respectively. Since the myelin sheath serves to accelerate axonal conduction, damage to the myelin sheath greatly reduces the speed of axonal conduction. The prototype demyelination disorder of the CNS is multiple sclerosis. Individuals who suffer from multiple sclerosis experience intermittent bouts of motor weakness, impaired vision, and tremor. A demyelination of axons of the PNS occurs in a condition known as Guillain-Barré Syndrome. This condition is a mild respiratory infection that produces lower and upper limb weakness.*

| ○ Bipolar neuroblast | A | ○ Oligodendrocyte | C | ○ Protoplasmic astrocyte | E |
| ○ Multipolar neuroblast | B | ○ Ependymal cell | D | ○ Fibrous astrocyte | F |

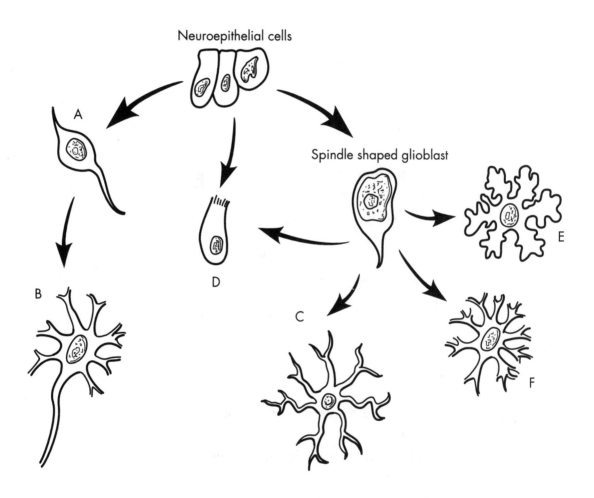

Neuroepithelial cells

A

Spindle shaped glioblast

B

D

E

C

F

THE DEVELOPING CENTRAL NERVOUS SYSTEM
self assessment

In this and every subsequent self-assessment in this book, the question format is that of extended matching. A list of choices is given at the top, with questions at the bottom. Match the question with the appropriate choice. Note that the choices outnumber the questions. Each letter may be used once, more than once, or not at all. Good Luck!

A. Alar plate
B. Cervical flexure
C. Cephalic flexure
D. Neural tube
E. Telencephalon
F. Myelencephalon
G. Metencephalon
H. Mesencephalon
I. Choroid plexus
J. Rhombic lips
K. Third ventricle
L. Optic vesicle
M. Lamina terminalis
N. Cerebral aqueduct
O. Lateral ventricle
P. Basal plate

1. Site of cerebrospinal fluid production

2. Stalk of this structure is the optic nerve

3. Gives rise to the cerebellum

4. Anterior boundary of structure that gives rise to entire CNS

5. Neurons of this structure give rise to dorsal horn of spinal cord

CHAPTER TWO

the
meninges

Chapter 2-1: The Meninges

The CNS, which includes the brain and spinal cord, is covered by three membranes: the outermost **dura mater (A)**, the innermost **pia mater (B)**, and the middle **arachnoid (C)**, which is in-between the other two membranes. The two innermost layers, arachnoid and pia, are often collectively referred to as the leptomeninges. The dura mater is the strongest of all three, and is bilayered; its outer **periostial layer (A₁)** adheres to the undersurface of the cranium and its inner **meningeal layer (A₂)** is continuous with the dura layer, which covers the spinal cord. The inner meningeal layer gives rise to the **falx cerebri (D)**, which divides the two cerebral hemispheres.

[Color A-C different colors. Color A, A₁, and A₂ different shades of the same color.]

The meningeal layer also gives rise to the tentorium cerebelli, which is not shown. The tentorium cerebelli separates the cerebellum from the cerebral hemispheres and allows communication between these two compartments through a structure called the tentorial incisure (not shown). The venous sinuses, one of which is the **dural sinus (E)**, lie in-between the two layers of the dura mater. They collect the venous drainage and cerebrospinal fluid of the brain and drain into the internal jugular veins of the neck. The dura mater receives its blood supply from the middle meningeal artery, which is a branch of the maxillary artery.

The pia mater is the layer that is most intimately adherent to the brain and spinal cord; so much so that it closely follows the brain's contours. This vascular membrane forms the tela choroidea and the choroid plexus. In areas where vessels enter or exit the brain, the pia invaginates to form a space between itself and the vessel called the **perivascular space (F)**.

[Color F, G, and H dark colors.]

The arachnoid is for the most part avascular and lies between the dura and the pia; it is separated from the dura by the **subdural space (G)**, and from the pia by the **subarachnoid space (H)**. The arachnoid and pia are both composed of loose connective tissue. The arachnoid is bound to the pia by the weblike **arachnoid trabeculae (I)**. The arachnoid also travels along the cranial and spinal nerve roots. The subarachnoid space is the compartment that harbors the circulating cerebrospinal fluid; it is in direct communication with the fourth ventricle via three foramina: the foramen of Magendie and the paired foramina of Luschka.

Clinical Correlates: *There is potentially a space between the dura and the cranium; it is known as a "potential" space because it does not really exist unless there is pathology. For instance, a strong blow to the side of the head could cause a laceration of the middle meningeal artery, which would lead to blood accumulation in the space that was created. This is known as an epidural hematoma. A blow to the front or back of the head, or a sudden stop from acceleration is also dangerous. For example, if someone were to run straight into a brick wall, head first, the sudden stop might cause a shearing force on the vessels of the brain as a result of the brain swaying back and forth in the head. The vessels that were affected would most likely be the veins that exit the brain parenchyma and drain into the dural sinus. These vessels would be subject to a shearing force and tear, producing an accumulation of blood in the subdural space—or a subdural hematoma. The danger of intracranial hematomas are that they grow in size and exert a pressure on the underlying brain that is potentially fatal.*

○ Dura mater	A	○ Meningeal layer	A₂	○ Subdural space	G
○ Pia mater	B	○ Falx cerebri	D	○ Subarachnoid space	H
○ Arachnoid	C	○ Dural sinus	E	○ Arachnoid trabeculae	I
○ Periostial layer	A₁	○ Perivascular space	F		

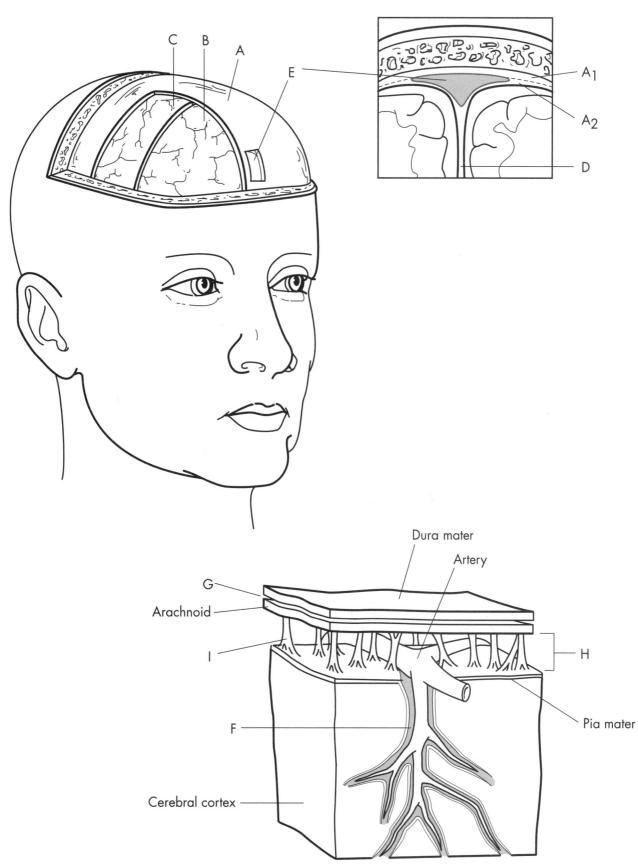

Dura mater

Artery

G

Arachnoid

I

H

F

Pia mater

Cerebral cortex

THE MENINGES
self assessment

A. Dura mater
B. Arachnoid
C. Pia mater
D. Falx cerebri
E. Subdural space
F. Perivascular space
G. Subarachnoid space
H. Arachnoid trabeculae
I. Foramen of Magendie
J. Foramen of Luschka

1. Area of cerebrospinal fluid circulation

2. This membrane is bilayered

3. Divides cerebral hemispheres

4. Structure separated from the brain's outermost covering by subdural space

5. Shearing of bridging veins initially causes bleeding into this compartment

CHAPTER THREE

the cerebral hemispheres

Chapter 3-1: Topography

The surface of the brain is full of sulci and gyri. Three sulci—the **central sulcus (A)**, **lateral sulcus (B)**, and **parieto-occipital sulcus (C)**—divide the cerebrum into its four lobes: the **frontal (D)**, **parietal (E)**, **temporal (F)**, and **occipital lobes (G)**.

[Trace the sulci using dark colors, and use light colors to color in the gyri.]

The frontal lobe extends from the frontal pole to the central sulcus and lies anterosuperior to the lateral sulcus. At the bottom of the lateral sulcus is an area of cortex known as the **insula (H)**, which can only be seen if the lateral sulcus is opened. The superolateral surface of the frontal lobe contains three major sulci—the **precentral sulcus (I)**, the **superior frontal sulcus (J)**, and the **inferior frontal sulcus (J₁)**—which divide the lobe into 4 gyri: the **precentral gyrus (K)**, the **superior frontal gyrus (L)**, the **middle frontal gyrus (L₁)**, and the **inferior frontal gyrus (L₂)**.

[Trace J and J₁ in different shades of the same color. Color L, L₁, and L₂ different shades of the same color.]

The parietal lobe lies posterior to the central sulcus, superior to the lateral sulcus, and extends posteriorly to the parietooccipital sulcus. Its lateral surface consists of two major sulci—the **postcentral sulcus (M)** and the **intraparietal sulcus**

(N)—and three major gyri: the **postcentral gyrus (O)**, the **superior parietal lobule (P)**, and the **inferior parietal lobule (P₁)**.

The temporal lobe lies inferior to the lateral sulcus and is divided by two sulci—the **superior temporal sulcus (Q)** and the **inferior temporal sulcus (Q₁)**—into three gyri: the **superior temporal gyrus (R)**, the **middle temporal gyrus (R₁)**, and the **inferior temporal gyrus (R₂)**. The occipital lobe lies posterior to the parietooccipital sulcus.

[Trace all of the Q's different shades of the same color; do the same when coloring all of the P's and R's.]

The frontal lobe contains the prefrontal area, which is involved in motor planning, concentration, and affective behavior; it also contains the motor area, which is involved in the processing and execution of motor function. The parietal lobe contains the primary somatosensory area, which receives sensory input from the body.

The temporal lobe is made up of a lateral and medial portion; the lateral portion serves as the primary sensory area for auditory and vestibular input, and the medial portion is involved in memory. The occipital lobe serves as the visual cortex.

thalamus - sensory relay center
hypo thalamus - homeostasis in body, drives (thirst)
cerebellum - fine motor coordination
basal ganglia - sustaining or initiating mvmt

inside Sylvian fissure = insular cortex - olfaction (+ possibly speech motor programming) neglect on L

lesion on P

○ Central sulcus	A	○ Inferior frontal sulcus	J₁	○ Superior parietal lobule *attention, proprioseption (esp. on right)*	P
○ Lateral sulcus	B	○ Precentral gyrus *primary motor cortex*	K	○ Inferior parietal lobule	P₁
○ Parieto-occipital sulcus	C	○ Superior frontal gyrus	L	○ Superior temporal sulcus	Q
○ Frontal lobe	D	○ Middle frontal gyrus	L₁	○ Inferior temporal sulcus	Q₁
○ Parietal lobe	E	○ Inferior frontal gyrus *Broca's - lang. production/expression*	L₂	○ Superior temporal gyrus *auditory cortex* *post. ⅓ = Wernicke's - lang comprehension*	R
○ Temporal lobe	F	○ Postcentral sulcus *somatosensory cortex - touch, pain proprioception, temperature*	M	○ Middle temporal gyrus *auditory/lang.*	R₁
○ Occipital lobe *vision*	G	○ Intraparietal sulcus	N	○ Inferior temporal gyrus *word meaning (esp. left side)*	R₂
○ Insula	H	○ Postcentral gyrus	O		
○ Precentral sulcus	I				
○ Superior frontal sulcus	J				

occipital temporal gyrus (fusiform) - face recognition

Limbic Lobe (medial) - emotion, learning
Cingulate Gyrus (medial) attention (anterior portion)
hippo campus - long term memory
amygdala - emotion - esp. fear

inf. middle & sup. frontal gyri - motor planning, working memory

proprioception, spatial perception

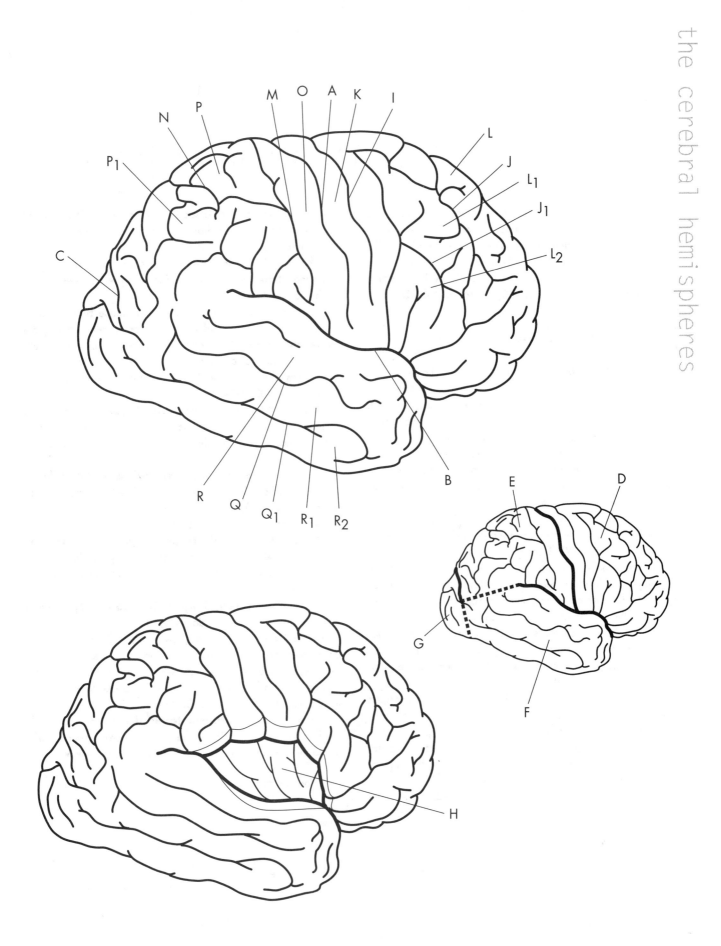

Chapter 3-2: Cellular Organization

The cerebral cortex is composed of nerve fibers, neuroglia, blood vessels, and over 10 billion neurons. It is organized into a six-layer cellular arrangement; the layers are numbered I-VI from the outermost to innermost portion of the cortex. The principal types of cells found in the cerebral cortex are as follows: **horizontal (A)**, **fusiform (B)**, **stellate (C)**, **pyramidal (D)**, and **Martinotti (E)**.

[Color A-E different colors.]

Neurons of each layer have certain functional characteristics. Layers I, II, and III are responsible for most of the intracortical association functions. Layer IV is the first to receive sensory input; from here the sensory input travels to other areas of the cortex. Layer V neurons contain axons that extend to more distant parts of the cortex, such as the thalamus and brain stem.

One example of fusiform cells are the cells of Cajal, which lie horizontally in the cortex and have long axons that also run horizontally. They are located in layer I, the most superficial layer of the cortex.

Most of the fusiform cells, however, are found in the deepest cortical layer; layer VI. Dendrites project from each of the fusiform cell's poles; the inferior dendrite arborizes within the same layer, while the superior dendrite projects to the surface layers. The fusiform cell's axon emerges from its inferior portion, and enters the white matter as a projection fiber.

The small stellate cells (also called granule cells) are polygonal in shape; they are made up of multiple dendrites and a short axon. They occupy all layers of the cerebral cortex, but are especially abundant in layer IV.

The pyramidal cells have pyramid shaped bodies. Their apex is pointed towards the superficial surface, and from it arises a thick dendrite that extends toward the pia. This projection is known as the apical dendrite. From its inferior aspect arise basal dendrites that project semi-horizontally to arborize with its immediate neighbors. Its axon arises from the base of the cell body and either projects into the deep cortex, or travels to the white matter as a projection or association fiber. There is also a giant variant of pyramidal cell that is found in the precentral gyrus of the frontal lobe and is called the Betz cell.

The cells of Martinotti are small multipolar cells whose axons are oriented towards the surface. They are present in essentially all the cortical layers.

Each layer of the cerebral cortex is unique because of its type, its arrangement, and the density of its cells. Layer I, the **molecular layer (F)**, is the most superficial and contains cells with horizontally oriented axons. It also contains the dendritic projections of the pyramidal and fusiform cells and the axonal terminations of the cells of Martinotti.

Layer II, the **external granular layer (G)**, contains a number of tightly-packed stellate cells. Their dendrites terminate in the molecular layer and their axons enter the deep cortical layers.

Layer III, the **external pyramidal layer (H)**, is full of medium-sized and large pyramidal cells. Their dendrites travel to the molecular layer, and their axons enter the white matter as projection or association fibers.

Layer IV, the **internal granular layer (I)**, is packed with stellate cells. Also present in this layer is a layer of horizontally organized, myelinated fibers known collectively as the external band of Baillarger.

Layer V, the **internal pyramidal layer (J)**, contains medium and large pyramidal cells, stellate cells, and cells of Martinotti. Dendrites of the large pyramidal cells enter the molecular layer, those of the small pyramidal cells extend as high as layer IV, and the axons enter the white matter mainly as projection fibers. This layer also contains a horizontal fiber arrangement called the inner band of Baillarger.

Layer VI, the **multiform layer (K)**, contains primarily small and large fusiform cells. Their dendritic organization is similar to the one described for the pyrmidal cells in layer V.

[You can color layers F-K lightly, using different colors.]

○ Horizontal cell	A	○ Cells of Martinotti	E	○ Internal granular layer	I
○ Fusiform cell	B	○ Molecular layer	F	○ Internal pyramidal layer	J
○ Stellate cell	C	○ External granular layer	G	○ Multiform layer	K
○ Pyramidal cells	D	○ External pyramidal layer	H		

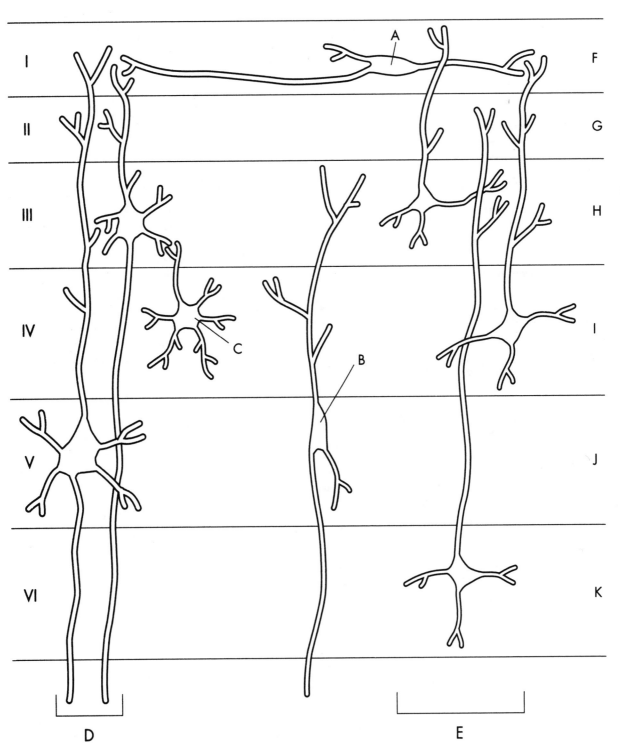

I

II

III

IV

V

VI

A

F

G

H

I

J

K

C

B

D

E

Chapter 3-3: Specialized Cortical Areas: Motor System

The cerebral cortex is divided into functional regions that are differentiated based on their cytological architecture. These areas are known as Brodmann's areas, and there are 52 of them in all; most of them are illustrated on the accompanying page. We will discuss the major ones in detail.

The * (A) is designated Brodmann's area 4 and is located in the posterior half of the precentral gyrus. As you can see, the parts of the body are topographically organized on specific areas of the primary motor cortex; the leg and foot extend into the longitudinal fissure and the face is at the bottom, near the lateral sulcus. Why, you may ask, are the different parts of the body so variable in size on the homunculus? That's a fair question. The answer is that the those parts of the body that require a greater skill and precision of movement will have a greater portion of the primary motor cortex devoted to them. For instance, fingers require fine motor coordination (i.e. for playing piano, picking up objects, or threading a needle) and, therefore, since more skill is involved in such movements, the hand and fingers are allotted a generous portion of the primary motor cortex. Conversely, the muscles of the trunk are not required to carry out fine and highly skilled movements and, as a result, make up a smaller portion of the primary motor cortex. The execution of control of the primary cortex on the different parts of the body can be described in the following way: stimulating one point in the hand area of the primary motor cortex leads to the contraction of a single muscle (or even a portion of a muscle) of the hand, whereas, stimulating one point of the trunk region on the primary motor cortex results in the stimulation of a group of muscles. As you can see, it is for a good reason that the detail to which the hand muscles are represented on the primary motor cortex is much greater than that of the trunk muscles. The motor homunculus shows in great detail the degree to which each part of the body is repre-

sented in the primary motor cortex. So as you can see, the primary motor cortex carries out the movement of different parts of the body, but in doing so, it receives assistance (in the form of input) from the premotor area, sensory cortex, basal ganglia, thalamus, and cerebellum.

The * (B) is Brodmann's area 6, and it primarily occupies the anterior half of the precentral gyrus. It works in concert with the primary motor area, basal ganglia, and thalamus. For instance, if the premotor area were required to effect the movement of a specific part of the body, it would send a signal to the basal ganglia and this signal would then travel to the thalamus and back to the primary motor cortex; but the premotor area could also send a signal directly to the primary motor cortex.

The * (C) lies superior to the premotor area and drops into the longitudinal fissure, as can be seen on the cross-sectional diagram. Stimulation of this area usually results in bilateral muscular contractions, as opposed to unilateral contractions; a stronger stimulus to this area is required to produce total muscular contraction.

[Color A, B, and C different shades of the same color; make A the darkest of the shades, and the others lighter shades.]

○ Primary motor cortex   A   ○ Premotor area   B   ○ Supplementary motor area   C

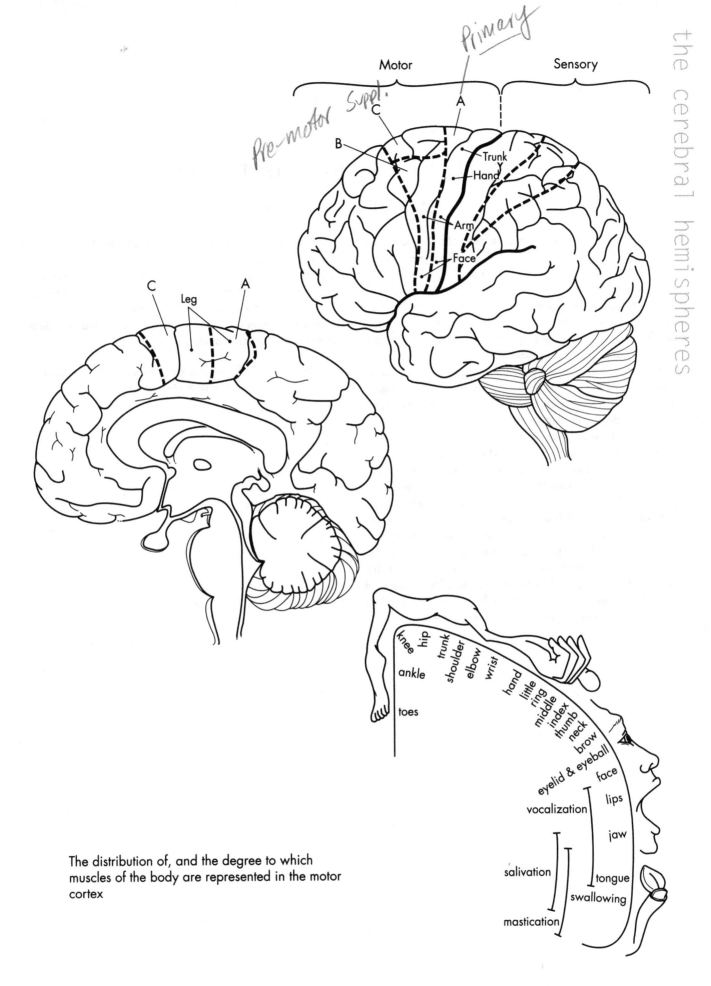

Motor

Sensory

Primary

Pre-motor   Suppl.

C

A

B

Trunk

Hand

Arm

Face

C   Leg   A

knee
hip
trunk
shoulder
elbow
wrist
ankle
hand
little
ring
middle
index
thumb
neck
brow
toes
eyelid & eyeball
face
vocalization
lips
jaw
salivation
tongue
swallowing
mastication

The distribution of, and the degree to which muscles of the body are represented in the motor cortex

Chapter 3-4: Specialized Cortical Areas: Sensory System

The **primary somatosensory cortex (A)** is made up of Brodmann's areas 3, 1, and 2, and is located in the postcentral gyrus. This area receives sensory input from the thalamic ventral posterior lateral and medial nuclei (VPL and VPM, respectively). Most of the sensory input that it receives comes from the opposite side of the body. Almost all sensory impulses, with the exception of olfactory impulses, travel to specific areas of the cerebral cortex via thalamocortical projections. In a way that's similar to the motor cortex, the sensory system can be topographically organized; see the homunculus of the postcentral gyrus that's shown on the accompanying page. The area allotted to each of the body parts in the diagram is directly proportional to the density of sensory receptors in those body parts. Since the lips occupy the greatest area in the sensory homunculus, you may deduce they must have the greatest number of sensory receptors—they do.

One way to determine the physiology of a particular area of the body is to examine the impact of excising the organ in question; for instance, the following are the results of excising the primary somatosensory cortex: (1) an inability to evaluate texture of materials, (2) an inability to determine shapes of objects (astereognosia), (3) an inability to accurately localize sensations that occur on a specific part of the body, (4) an inability to determine different degrees of pressure sensation. There is also a secondary somatosensory area, but its function remains unclear.

The **somatosensory association cortex (B)** is made up of Brodmann's areas 5 and 7 and is located in the superior parietal lobule. This area receives sensory input from the primary somatosensory cortex, thalamic nuclei, auditory cortex, and visual cortex; after receiving these signals, it integrates them. For instance, it allows us to hold an object in our hand and identify it using only our sense of touch.

[Color A and B different shades of the same color; make A the darker of the two shades.]

○ Primary somatosensory cortex   A   ○ Somatosensory association cortex   B

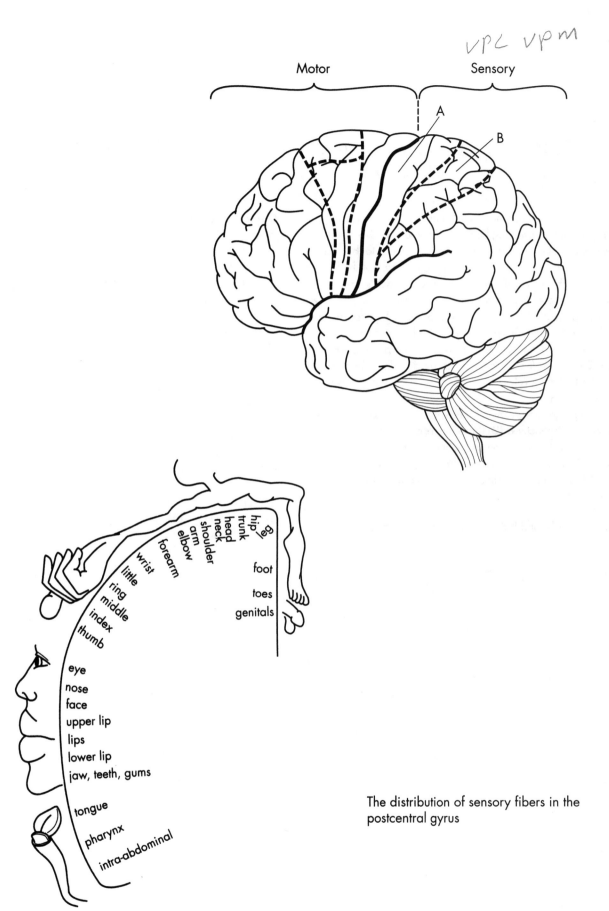

VPL VPM

Motor   Sensory

A

B

hip
trunk
head
neck
shoulder
arm
elbow
forearm
wrist
little
ring
middle
index
thumb

leg
foot
toes
genitals

eye
nose
face
upper lip
lips
lower lip
jaw, teeth, gums
tongue
pharynx
intra-abdominal

The distribution of sensory fibers in the
postcentral gyrus

Chapter 3-5: Specialized Cortical Areas: Broca's and Wernicke's

The left cerebral hemisphere is the dominant hemisphere for language in most individuals, be they right or left-handed. The entire language system (or language zone) appears to be located around the lateral sulcus. Word formation is accomplished by the region of the cerebral cortex known as **Broca's area (A)** (Brodmann's area 44). It is located in the inferior portion of the left frontal gyrus. The initiation and execution of speech are controlled by this area. Since this area is involved with the execution of speech, it is fitting that it spills over into the premotor area. In fact, Broca's area produces speech by actually stimulating the muscles that are involved in speech (i.e. the laryngeal muscles) to contract.

Language interpretation and comprehension is accomplished by **Wernicke's area (B)** (Brodmann's area 22), which is located in the posterior portion of the superior temporal lobe. Since this area is involved with language comprehension, it is fitting that it lies behind the primary auditory cortex (this will be discussed later).

[Color A and B different shades of the same color.]

Clinical Correlates: An aphasia is an impairment in one's ability to speak or understand words, either spoken or written, due to a lesion in the brain. Difficulty in speaking words is an aphasia often termed expressive, motor, or Broca's aphasia—all three terms are used interchangeably. In this condition, the person has no problem mentally formulating the words and organizing them into a sentence, but when he tries to speak them, all that is heard is noise, rather than the words. The person is fully aware of what is happening and, thus, becomes frustrated. The lesion that causes this impairment is located in Broca's area. It should be understood that, like most other disorders, there are mild and severe forms of this aphasia; in the milder form of Broca's aphasia, the person may be able to speak some sentences but may place the accent on the wrong syllables, for instance.

Another type of aphasia is marked by the inability to comprehend the meaning of words; written or spoken. Different terms are also applied to this type of aphasia: receptive, sensory, or Wernicke's aphasia. In this condition, the person has no problem speaking words, but his spoken words are jumbled and meaningless, and not in an intelligible order in a sentence. People with this type of aphasia seem to be unaware of their problem and do not understand anything that is said to them.

○ Broca's area   A   ○ Wernicke's area   B

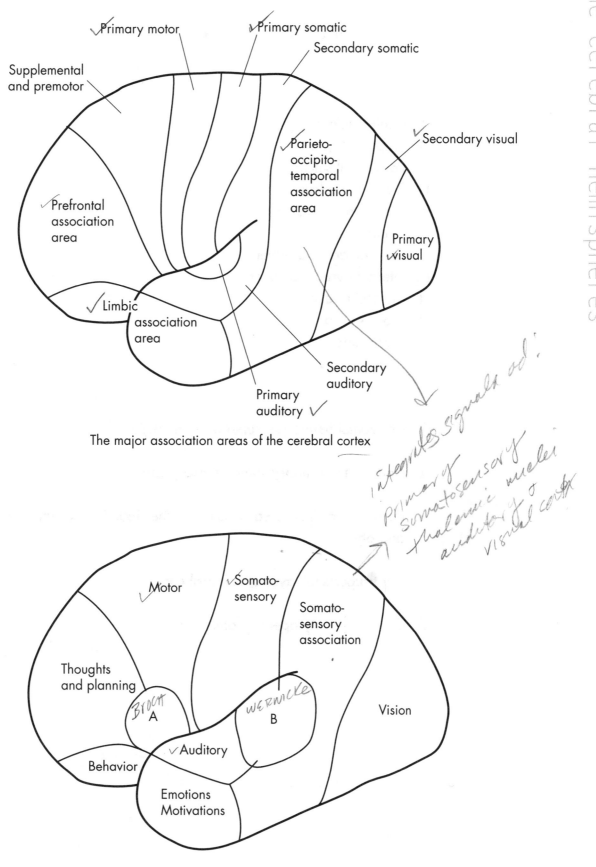

The major association areas of the cerebral cortex

Specific functional areas in the cerebral cortex

THE CEREBRAL HEMISPHERES

self assessment

A. Central sulcus
B. Precentral gyrus
C. Postcentral sulcus
D. Precentral sulcus
E. Postcentral gyrus
F. Insula
G. External granular layer
H. Internal pyramidal layer
I. Molecular layer
J. Broca's area
K. Wernicke's area
L. Lateral sulcus

1. Horizontal fissure just superior to temporal lobe

2. Harbors the primary somatosensory cortex

3. Damage to this area results in the inability to understand words and phrases

4. Most superficial layer of cerebral cortex

5. Can be seen by opening lateral sulcus

the
cranial
nerves

Chapter 4-1: An Overview

There are 12 pairs of cranial nerves; they are numbered in order from the anterior to the posterior part of the brain. Each of these pairs of cranial nerves passes through a specific foramen, or opening, in the skull, and 10 of the 12 originate from the brain stem. Some of the nerves contain only sensory fibers, while others contain motor fibers and the rest contain both sensory and motor fibers; they are respectively known as sensory, motor, and mixed nerves. The cell bodies of sensory fibers are located outside the brain, but the cell bodies of motor fibers are found within specific nuclei within the brain—these nuclei are called the cranial nerve nuclei.

[Color each of the cranial nerves a different color.]

The 12 cranial nerves are as follows:

   I: **Olfactory (A)**
  II: **Optic (B)**
 III: **Oculomotor (C)**
 IV: **Trochlear (D)**
  V: **Trigeminal (E)**
 VI: **Abducens (F)**
 VII: **Facial (G)**
VIII: **Vestibulocochlear (H)**
 IX: **Glossopharyngeal (I)**
  X: **Vagus (J)**
 XI: **Spinal Accessory (K)**
XII: **Hypoglossal (L)**

The olfactory, optic, and vestibulocochlear nerves are purely sensory. The oculomotor, trochlear, abducens, spinal accessory, and hypoglossal nerves are purely motor. The trigeminal, facial, glossopharyngeal, and vagus are mixed nerves; they contain both sensory and motor fibers. Remembering this information can be difficult, so here are a couple of mnemonic devices that might be helpful; the first of these will help you remember the cranial nerves in the correct order, and the second one will help you recall which cranial nerves are sensory (S), which are motor (M), and which are both (B).

Oh, **O**h, **O**h, **T**o, **T**ouch, **A**nd, **F**eel, **V**ery, **G**reen, **V**egetable, **A**, **H**

Some, **S**ay, **M**arry, **M**oney, **B**ut, **M**y, **B**rother, **S**ays, **B**etter, **B**rains, **M**atter, **M**ore

○	Olfactory nerve	A	○	Abducens nerve	F	○	Vagus nerve	J
○	Optic nerve	B	○	Facial nerve	G	○	Spinal accessory nerve	K
○	Oculomotor nerve	C	○	Vestibulocochlear nerve	H	○	Hypoglossal nerve	L
○	Trochlear nerve	D	○	Glossopharyngeal nerve	I			
○	Trigeminal nerve	E						

Distribution of cranial nerves

Chapter 4-2: Location and Foramina

On pages 38-39 is a chart that summarizes the characteristics of the cranial nerves; the first column lists the name of the nerve, the second column lists the type of fibers that make up the nerve (motor, sensory, or both), the third lists the foramen through which the nerve passes, and the fourth column contains an abbreviated list of the nerve's functions

Here are a couple of ways to remember the locations of the cranial nerves. First divide the base of the brain into 3 parts, making pons central. Now you have the area anterior to the pons (part 1), the pons themselves (part 2), and the area posterior to the pons (part 3). The cranial nerves that lie anterior to the basilar pons are cranial nerves I-III, and those that lie in or adjacent to the pons are cranial nerves IV-VIII; those lying posterior to the pons are cranial nerves IX-XII. This organization should make sense to you because, as we stated earlier, the cranial nerves are numbered in order going from the anterior to the posterior part of the brain.

[Color each cranial nerve the same color (or a different shade of the same color) as the foramen through which it passes.]

○ Cribriform plate	A	○ Foramen rotundum	E_2	○ Internal acoustic meatus	H_1
○ Optic nerve	B	○ Foramen ovale	E_3	○ Glossopharyngeal nerve	I
○ Optic canal	B_1	○ Abducens nerve	F		
○ Oculomotor nerve	C	○ Facial nerve	G	○ Jugular foramen	I_1
○ Superior orbital fissure	C_1	○ Internal acoustic meatus	G_1	○ Vagus nerve	J
○ Trochlear nerve	D	○ Facial canal	G_2	○ Spinal accessory nerve	K
○ Superior orbital fissure	D_1	○ Stylomastoid foramen	G_3	○ Jugular foramen	K_1
○ Trigeminal nerve	E	○ Vestibulocochlear nerve	H	○ Hypoglossal nerve	L
○ Superior orbital fissure	E_1			○ Hypoglossal canal	L_1

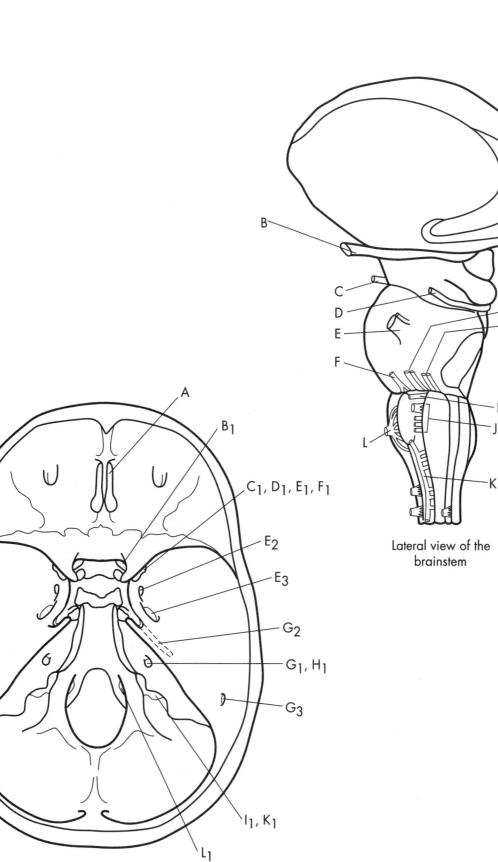

B

C
D
E
F

G
H

I
J

L

K

Lateral view of the
brainstem

A

B₁

C₁, D₁, E₁, F₁

E₂

E₃

G₂

G₁, H₁

G₃

I₁, K₁

L₁

Location of cranial nerves and foramina

Table of Cranial Nerve Locations and Foramina

NERVE	FIBERS	FORAMEN	FUNCTION
I Olfactory	Sensory	Cribriform Plate (A)	Smell
II Optic (B)	Sensory	Optic canal (B_1)	Vision
III Oculomotor (C)	Motor	Superior orbital fissure (C_1)	Moves eyes up, down, up/lateral
IV Trochlear (D)	Motor	Superior orbital fissure (D_1)	Moves eyes down/lateral
V Trigeminal (E) (3 divisions)	Both		
Ophthalmic	Sensory	Superior orbital fissure (E_1)	Carries info from the scalp, nasal mucosa, different parts of eye
Maxillary	Sensory	Foramen rotundum (E_2)	Carries info from the palate, upper lip, jaw, and teeth
Mandibular (sensory and motor)	Sensory part		Carries info from the lower jaw, teeth, salivary glands, and tongue
	Motor part	Foramen ovale (E_3)	Muscles of mastication
VI Abducens (F)	Motor	Superior orbital fissure (F_1)	Moves the eye lateral

NERVE	FIBERS	FORAMEN	FUNCTION
VII Facial (G) (2 divisions)	Both		
	Sensory part		Carries taste info from anterior 2/3 of tongue
	Motor part	Internal acoustic meatus (G_1), Facial canal (G_2), Stylomastoid foramen (G_3)	Facial and scalp muscles, digastric and stylohyoid muscles
	Secretomotor		Submandibular and sublingual salivary glands
VIII Vestibulocochlear (H) (2 divisions)	Sensory		
Vestibular part	Sensory	Internal acoustic meatus (H_1)	Carries info about equilibrium and position
Cochlear part	Sensory		Carries info about hearing
IX Glossopharyngeal (I)	Both		
	Sensory part		Carries taste info from anterior 2/3 of tongue
	Motor part	Jugular foramen (I_1)	Swallowing
	Secretomotor		Parotid gland secretion
X Vagus (J)	Both		
	Sensory		Carry info from external auditory meatus
	Motor	Jugular foramen (I_1)	Innervates muscles of pharynx and larynx
XI Spinal accessory (K)	Motor	Jugular foramen (K_1)	Innervates sternocleidomastoid and trapezius muscles
XII Hypoglossal (L)	Motor	Hypoglossal canal (L_1)	Innervates muscles of tongue

Chapter 4-3: CN I: Olfactory Nerve and Smell

The olfactory nerve (CN I) is involved in the sense of smell. It extends from the olfactory membrane, which is a specialized segment of epithelium that contains olfactory receptor cells and lies in the upper part of the nostrils. Mucus is secreted onto the olfactory membrane by the **olfactory glands (A)**, which are interspersed among the olfactory receptor cells. The **olfactory receptor cells (B)** are bipolar nerve cells that send out a dozen or so **olfactory cilia (C)** that enter the mucus of the nasal cavity; the basal ends of the olfactory receptor cells give rise to a thin, unmyelinated **olfactory axon (D)**. The cilia pick up the smell in the air and stimulate the olfactory cells, and the odor causes a depolarization of the olfactory membrane. The unmyelinated axons collectively penetrate a **Schwann cell (E)** envelope and enter the **cribriform plate (F)** as the olfactory nerve. Once they pass through the cribriform plate, they enter the anterior end of the **olfactory bulb (G)** on the other side. They terminate in specific rounded terminals in the olfactory bulb known as **glomeruli (H)**. Also terminating in the glomeruli are the dendrites of **mitral cells (I)** and **tufted cells (J)**, both of which send axons down into the **olfactory tract (K)**; these are basically the projection neurons of the olfactory bulb. The **granule cell (L)** receives excitatory input from the mitral cells and, in turn, feedback inhibits the mitral cells. The **periglomerular cell (M)** also inhibits mitral cells.

[Color A-M different colors. Color E and F light colors.]

Where the olfactory tract approaches the **anterior perforated substance (N)**, it divides into a **lateral olfactory stria (O)** and a **medial olfactory stria (P)**. The lateral olfactory stria projects to what are called the prepiriform and periamygdaloid regions; this area is known as the primary olfactory cortex. The medial olfactory stria contains fibers that cross the **anterior commissure (Q)** to enter the olfactory bulb on the opposite side, as well as fibers that enter the **subcallosal area (R)** and **septal nuclei (S)**.

[Color O and P different shades of the same color and color the other areas, blending between them.]

Clinical Correlates: *Skull fractures or olfactory groove meningiomas (types of brain tumor) may damage the olfactory nerve, resulting in a loss of smell. This is known as anosmia.*

○ Olfactory glands	A	○ Olfactory bulb	G	○ Anterior perforated substance	N
○ Olfactory receptor cells	B	○ Glomeruli	H	○ Lateral olfactory stria	O
○ Olfactory cilia	C	○ Mitral cells	I	○ Medial olfactory stria	P
○ Unmyelinated Olfactory axon	D	○ Tufted cells	J	○ Anterior commissure	Q
○ Schwann cell	E	○ Olfactory tract	K	○ Subcallosal area	R
○ Cribriform plate	F	○ Granule cell	L	○ Septal nuclei	S
		○ Periglomerular cell	M		

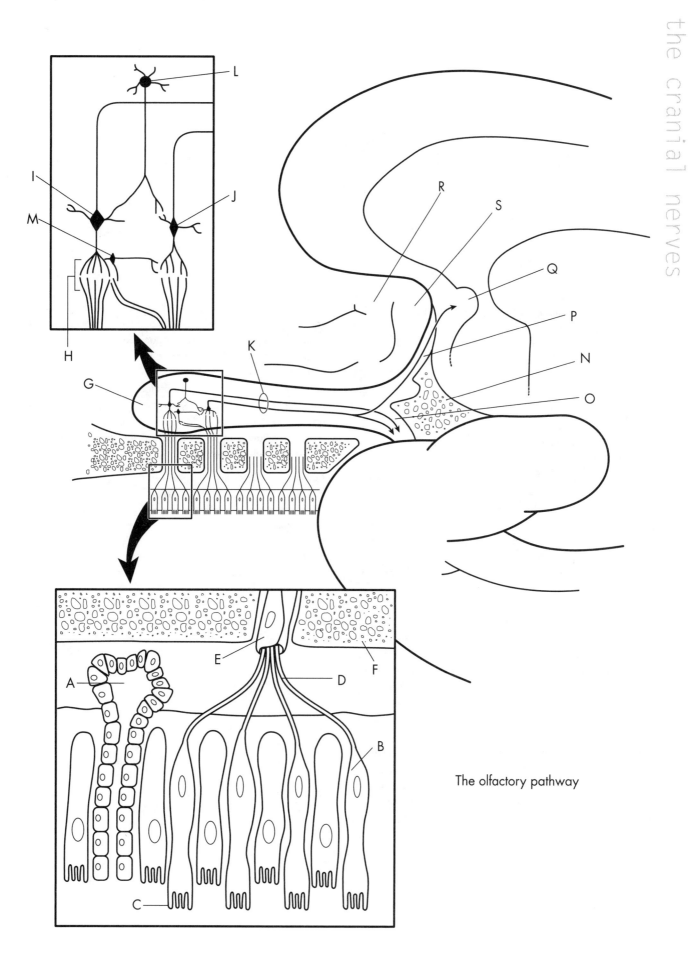

The olfactory pathway

Chapter 4-4: CN II: Optic Nerve and Visual Pathways

Vision is the domain of the optic nerve. The visual pathway will be discussed shortly. But first, a word on visual fields.

Let's divide the retina into nasal and temporal halves with respect to visual fields. The nasal half is the medial half, and the temporal half is the lateral half. The following point is extremely important: For each retina, the visual field of the nasal retina lies in the temporal direction, while the visual field of the temporal retina lies in the nasal direction. Therefore, the left visual field will be subserved by the left nasal retina and the right temporal retina, and the right visual field will be subserved by the right nasal retina and the left temporal retina. The temporal *retina* and the temporal *visual field* are *not* the same. For instance, the right temporal retina is simply the lateral side of the right retina. The right temporal *visual field* is that area of space seen by the nasal side of the right retina.

The **optic nerves (A)** arise as axons from the ganglionic layer of the retina, meet at the optic disk, and exit the orbit through the optic canals. Until they cross to form the **optic chiasm (B)**, they are known as optic nerves. After the chiasm, they continue and are called **optic tracts (C)**. Optic nerve fibers from the nasal half of each retina cross in the midline, just superior to the sella turcica, and enter the optic tract on the opposite side. The crossing zone is known as the optic chiasm.

The fibers from the temporal half do not cross; they enter the optic tract on the same side. The optic tract runs posteriorly around the **cerebral peduncles (D)** and synapse with the **lateral geniculate body (E)** of the thalamus on the same side. The lateral geniculate body relays visual information to the visual cortex (on the same side) via the **optic radiations (F)**, and also modulates the amount of information that passes to t he cortex (some fibers pass to the pretectal region and the superior colliculus, which is involved with visual reflexes).

Now, let's summarize these points. The left optic tract carries information from the left temporal retina and the right nasal retina (that crossed at the chiasm and entered the optic tract on the opposite side). The left optic tract then relays information to the ipsilateral (same side) lateral geniculate body, which, via the optic radiations, relays information to the ipsilateral occipital cortex. Therefore, the left occipital cortex sees the right side of the world, and vice versa.

[Color A, B, and C different shades of the same color.]

The **primary visual cortex (G)** is located in the calcarine fissure of the occipital lobes and is designated Brodmann's area 17. Visual information is organized in the occipital lobe in such a way that the signals coming from the central retina project to the occipital poles (the edge of the occipital lobes) and the signals from the peripheral retina project to areas more anterior to the occipital poles. Therefore, the more peripheral the visual signal, the more anterior (to the occipital poles) it will project. The visual association cortex lies around the primary visual cortex and is Brodmann's area 18.

Clinical Correlates: *Damage to a segment of the visual pathway will result in a visual field loss. For instance, a pituitary tumor that compresses the optic chiasm will result in the compression of the fibers crossing in the optic chiasm—fibers from the nasal retina of each eye. Now, what type of visual field defect would result from compression of nerve fibers of the nasal retina? You may recall that the visual field of the nasal retina is in the temporal direction. As a result, one's ability to see in the temporal field of vision will be impaired. This is called* bitemporal hemianopsia. *Note that the disorder is named according to the particular visual field lost, not the nerve fibers damaged. Therefore, this condition was not named binasal hemianopsia, because although it was the nasal fibers that were affected, the affected field of vision was the temporal field.*

Let's consider another example; say that the right optic tract (not optic nerve) becomes damaged. What visual field would be lost? Well, the right optic tract carries the nasal retinal fibers from the left retina and the temporal retinal fibers from the right retina. As a result, you would have a temporal visual field loss in the left eye and a nasal visual field loss in the right eye. This is known as a left homonymous hemianopsia. Conversely, a defect of the left optic tract would result in a right homonymous hemianopsia. Injury to an optic nerve causes blindness in the eye on the same side.

○ Optic nerve	A	○ Cerebral peduncle	D	○ Optic radiation	F
○ Optic chiasm	B	○ Lateral geniculate body	E	○ Primary visual cortex	G
○ Optic tract	C				

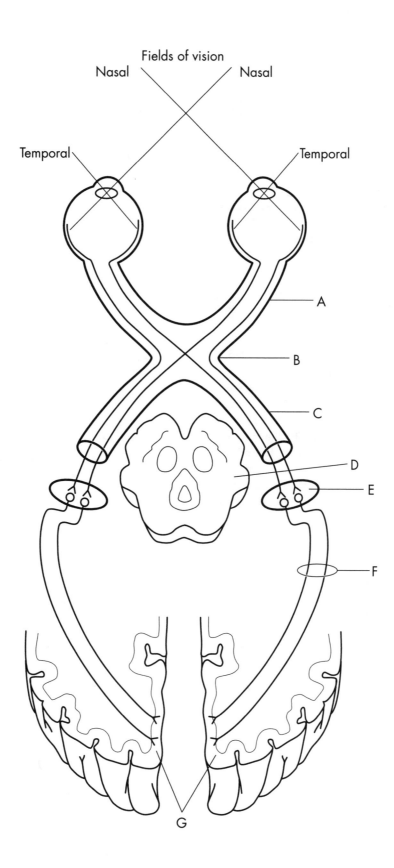

Fields of vision

Nasal   Nasal

Temporal   Temporal

A

B

C

D

E

F

G

The optic pathway

Chapter 4-5: CN II: The Retina

The retina is the light-sensitive structure of the eye and is involved in image formation. Its outer layer forms the pigmented epithelium, and its inner layer forms the neural portion. The neural portion consists of three layers of cells: a layer that contains the **rods (A)** and **cones (B)**, a layer of **bipolar cells (C)**, and a layer of **ganglion cells (D)**. Rods and cones are photoreceptors that are responsible for vision. Rods are very sensitive to light and permit vision even in dim light, while cones are suited for color and provide the sharpness of vision, but they require good lighting to function. The cones are concentrated in the fovea, which is a depression in the center of a region called the macula, which is an area located in the central retina. The macula contains the highest concentration of cones and, therefore, it is the area of sharpest visual acuity. The rods are located in increasing numbers as you move toward the periphery of the retina, and the cones decrease in number. The bipolar cells connect the rods and cones to the ganglion cells; they send axons into the optic nerve. The point where the optic nerve leaves the eye is called the optic disk, it can be visualized through an ophthalmoscope. This point is also known as the blind spot, because it contains no rods or cones. Other interlinking cells, in addition to the ones mentioned above, are the **horizontal cells (E)** and the **amacrine cells (F)**.

[Use different colors for A-F; make A a darker color than B.]

○ Rods	A	○ Bipolar cells	C	○ Horizontal cells	E
○ Cones	B	○ Ganglion cells	D	○ Amacrine cells	F

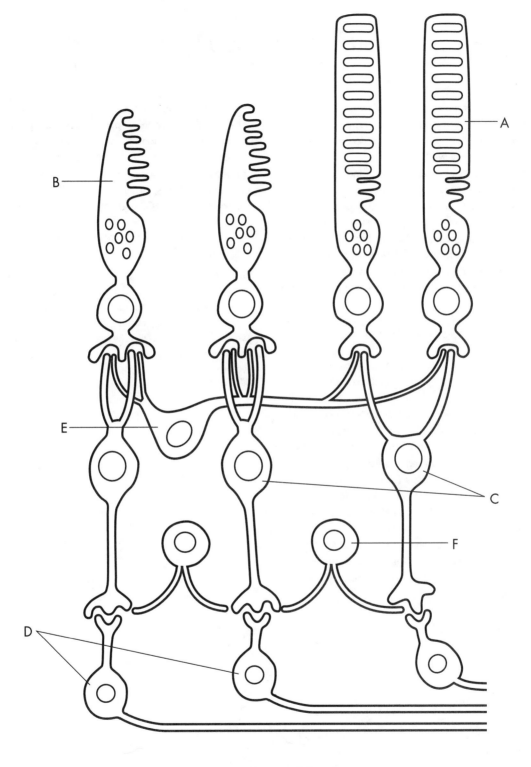

Anatomy of the retina

Chapter 4-6: CN III: Oculomotor Nerve

The oculomotor, trochlear, and abducens nerve are all involved in extraocular movements, or movements of the eye, and must work in concert. For this reason, they will be discussed in succession before we go on to cranial nerve V.

First, you should understand the muscles of the eye and how they work. The **lateral rectus (A)** moves the eye laterally, the **medial rectus (B)** moves the eye medially (this is known as adduction—movement toward the body), the **superior rectus (C)** moves the eye up and out, the **inferior rectus (D)** moves the eye down and out, the **superior oblique (E)** moves the eye down and in, the **inferior oblique (F)** moves the eye up and in. Another muscle, the **levator palpebrae superioris (G)** elevates the upper eyelid.

[Color A-G different colors.]

The **oculomotor nerve (H)** is a motor nerve that innervates the following muscles: the levator palpebrae superioris, the superior rectus, the inferior rectus, the medial rectus, and the inferior oblique. Essentially, it innervates all of the extraocular muscles except the lateral rectus and the superior oblique. The oculomotor nerve also sends parasympathetic nerve fibers to the **ciliary ganglion (I)**, which in turn sends parasympathetic fibers to the **sphincter pupillae muscles (J)** of the iris.

The **oculomotor nucleus (K)** lies ventrolateral to the cerebral aqueduct at the level of the **superior colliculus (L)**. It contains groups of nuclei that supply the extraocular muscles that are listed above. These fibers leave the nucleus and travel through tegmentum and red nucleus to the interpeduncular fossa. They then go on to enter the superior orbital fissure and innervate its specific muscles.

The oculomotor nerve also has an accessory motor nucleus, called the **Edinger-Westphal nucleus (M)**, which is located posterior to the oculomotor nucleus. It sends out parasympathetic fibers that enter the oculomotor nerve and travel to the ciliary ganglion. They synapse with other neurons that send fibers through the **ciliary nerves (N)**, which go on to innervate the **ciliary muscles (O)** and sphincter pupillae muscles.

[Color K and M different shades of the same color.]

Clinical Correlates: *Damage to the oculomotor nerve fibers often results in very defined symptoms. For instance, denervation (loss of innervation) of the medial rectus results in an eye that deviates laterally. This occurs because the action of the lateral rectus (which pulls the eye laterally) goes unopposed. Damage to the fibers innervating the levator palpebrae superioris would result in eye-droop, known as ptosis.*

○ Lateral rectus	A	○ Inferior oblique	F	○ Oculomotor nucleus	K
○ Medial rectus	B	○ Levator palpebrae superioris	G	○ Superior colliculus	L
○ Superior rectus	C	○ Oculomotor nerve	H	○ Edinger-Westphal nucleus	M
○ Inferior rectus	D	○ Ciliary ganglion	I	○ Ciliary nerves	N
○ Superior oblique	E	○ Sphincter pupillae muscles	J	○ Ciliary muscles	O

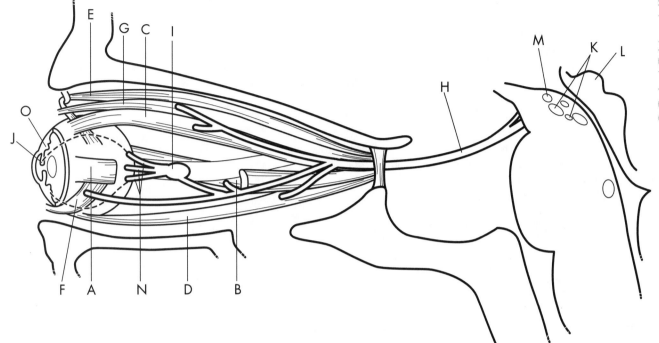

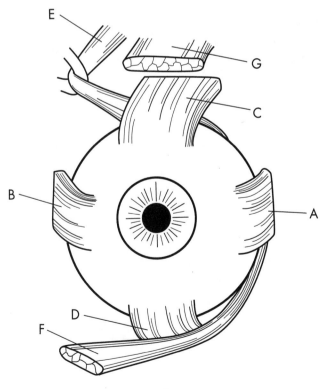

Left eye

Chapter 4-7: CN IV: Trochlear Nerve

The trochlear nerve innervates the **superior oblique (A)** muscle of the eye. Its nucleus is located just caudal to the **oculomotor nucleus (B)**, at the level of the **inferior colliculus (C)**. The trochlear nerve is unique in its course: it passes dorsally around the cerebral aqueduct, crosses in the superior medullary vellum, and emerges on the posterior aspect of the midbrain, just below the inferior colliculus. It is the only nerve that leaves the dorsal surface of the brain stem, and from this point, it travels anteriorly around the cerebral peduncle, through the lateral wall of the cavernous sinus, and then enters the orbit through the superior orbital fissure, to reach the superior oblique muscle.

[Color A, B, and C different colors.]

Clinical Correlates: *A lesion of the trochlear nerve would affect the one muscle it innervates—the superior oblique. Recall that the superior oblique muscle moves the eye down and in. As a result, damage to the trochlear nerve would weaken the downward movement of the eye when the eye was turned inward. This would cause the patient to have double vision (diplopia), and since the defect is in movement in the vertical direction, it is known as vertical diplopia. Damage to the trochlear nerve is the most common cause of symptomatic vertical diplopia. One clear symptom of this disorder is that the patient may complain of a difficulty in descending stairs. In this defect, patients often tilt their head to the opposite side in an attempt to compensate for the diplopia.*

○ Superior oblique   A   ○ Oculomotor nucleus   B   ○ Inferior colliculus   C

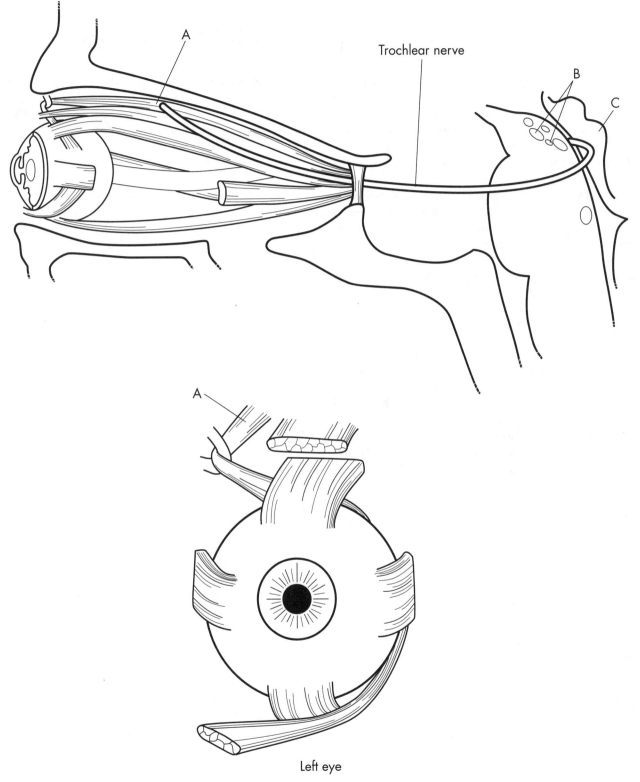

A

Trochlear nerve

B

C

A

Left eye

Chapter 4-8: CN VI: Abducens Nerve

As we stated earlier, cranial nerve VI is discussed contemporaneously with cranial nerves III and IV (and before cranial nerve V) since III, IV, and VI all have similar functions.

The abducens nerve innervates the **lateral rectus (A)** muscle of the eye, which moves the eye laterally. This is known as abduction—the movement in a direction away from the body. The **abducens nucleus (B)** is located in the pons, near the midline and beneath the floor of the fourth ventricle. The abducens nerve leaves its nucleus and travels anteriorly through the pons to emerge in the pontomedullary junction. From here it ascends anterior to the pons and passes over the apex of the petrous part of the temporal bone, through the lateral wall of the cavernous sinus, and finally through the superior orbital fissure to innervate the lateral rectus muscle.

[Color A and B different colors.]

A mnemonic device that will help you remember which particular eye muscle(s) is/are innervated by cranial nerves III, IV, and VI is the following: LR6(SO4)3. LR stands for lateral rectus, and it is innervated by cranial nerve 6. SO stands for superior oblique, and it is innervated by cranial nerve 4. The remaining muscles of the eye are innervated by cranial nerve 3. Note that the cranial nerves are usually represented by roman numerals, and were represented by numbers here only to illustrate the mnemonic.

Clinical Correlates: Damage to the abducens nerve causes a dysfunction of the lateral rectus. This results in the following: (1) an inability to abduct the eye, and (2) medial deviation of the eye due to unopposed medial rectus action.

○ Lateral rectus　　　　　　　　　　　A　　　　　　○ Abducens nucleus　　　　　　　　B

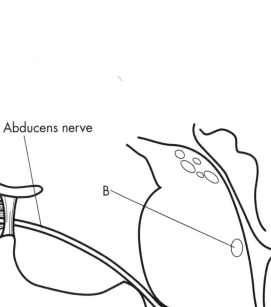

Abducens nerve

A

B

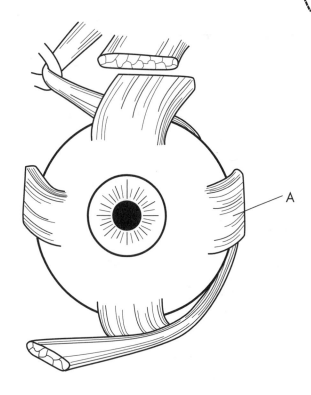

Left eye

A

Chapter 4-9: CN V: Trigeminal Nerve

The trigeminal nerve is the largest of all the cranial nerves; it contains both sensory and motor nerve fibers. It carries sensory information from most of the head (sense of pain, temperature, touch, and position), and provides motor innervation to the muscles of mastication (chewing).

Sensory neurons arise from cell bodies that are located in the **trigeminal ganglion (A)** (also known as the semilunar ganglion). From here, sensory fibers travel along three divisions of the trigeminal nerve: (1) the **ophthalmic division (B)**, (2) the **maxillary division (C)**, and (3) the **mandibular division (D)**. The ophthalmic division runs through the cavernous sinus and enters the orbit via the superior orbital fissure to innervate the upper portion of the face. Its sensory fibers terminate in the inferior portion of the **spinal trigeminal nucleus (E)**; this nucleus spans the medulla oblongata (and extends into the cervical spinal cord), and is the inferior extension of the **principal sensory nucleus (F)**, which is located in the dorsal pons. The maxillary division courses through the cavernous sinus, exits the cranium through the foramen rotundum, crosses the pterygopalatine fossa, and finally travels to the base of the orbit via the inferior orbital fissure to innervate the middle portion of the face. Its sensory fibers terminate in the mid-portion of the spinal trigeminal nucleus. The mandibular division is the largest branch of the trigeminal nerve; in addition to its sensory root, it contains the motor root of the trigeminal nerve. The sensory root does not traverse the cavernous sinus; it exits the cranium through the foramen ovale to innervate the lower portion of the face. Its sensory fibers terminate in the superior portion of the spinal nucleus.

[Color A-D different shades of the same color.]

Some sensory fibers leave the trigeminal ganglion and ascend to the principal sensory nucleus, which handles information about pressure and touch. Others descend to the spinal trigeminal nucleus, which relays information about pain and temperature, as well as touch. Proprioceptive nerve fibers arise from cell bodies of the **mesencephalic nucleus (G)**, a column of cells located in the gray matter that surrounds the cerebral aqueduct. The axons of the proprioceptive fibers innervate the muscles of mastication and travel to the trigeminal ganglion. Axons from the principal sensory and spinal trigeminal nuclei cross the brain stem, and with the trigeminal lemniscus, terminate in the ventral posteromedial (VPM) nucleus of the thalamus. These axons then travel in the internal capsule to the somatosensory cortex (the postcentral gyrus; areas 3,1,2 of the cerebral cortex).

[Color E-G different shades of the same color.]

The motor nerve fibers arise from the motor nucleus, which lies in the pons, medial to the principal sensory nucleus. These fibers cross through the brachium pontis and pass underneath the trigeminal ganglion to join the mandibular division of the trigeminal nerve, which contains the motor root. With the mandibular division, it enters the skull via the foramen ovale to innervate the following muscles: the **masseter (H)**, the **temporalis (I)**, the **pterygoids (J)**, and the **tensor tympani (K)**. The masseter, temporalis, and medial pterygoid muscles act to close the mandible (jaw). The lateral pterygoid muscle allows the mandible to open and move from side to side. The tensor tympani muscle dampens the vibration of the tympanic membrane (eardrum) in responsive to excessive sound.

[Color H-K different shades of red and pink.]

Clinical Correlates: *A well-known clinical condition associated with the trigeminal nerve is trigeminal neuralgia. It is a condition that causes transient, but severe, pain, mostly in the second and third (maxillary and mandibular) branches of the trigeminal nerve; it usually affects only one side of the face and does not result in a loss of sensory or motor function. The cause of this condition is unknown.*

○ Trigeminal gangion	A	○ Spinal trigeminal division	E	○ Masseter	H
○ Ophthalmic division	B			○ Temporalis	I
○ Maxillary division	C	○ Principal sensory nucleus	F	○ Pterygoids	J
○ Mandibular division	D	○ Mesencephalic nucleus	G	○ Tensor tympani	K

The pons

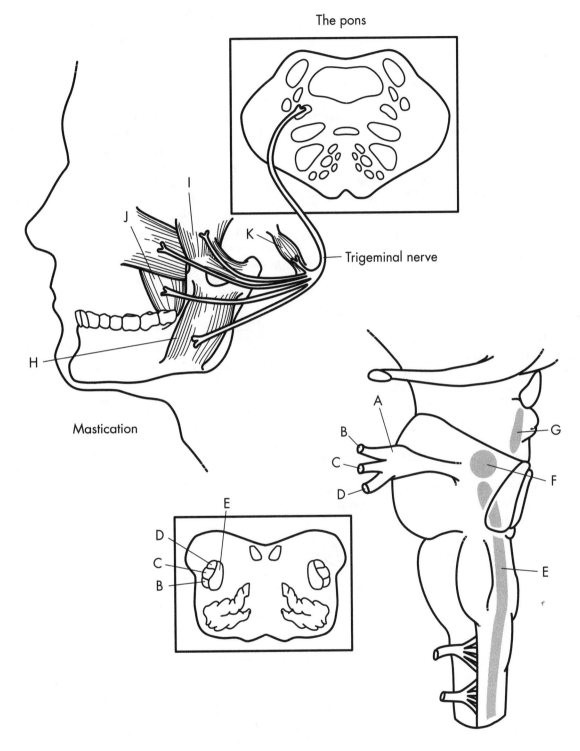

Trigeminal nerve

Mastication

Spinal trigeminal tract

Chapter 4-10: CN VII: Facial Nerve

The **facial nerve (A)** contains sensory, motor, and parasympathetic nerve fibers. Its sensory component is a small segment called the **nervus intermedius (B)**; this segment mediates taste that's received from the anterior two-thirds of the tongue. Its motor component innervates certain muscles, including the muscles of facial expression; the stapedius, the auricular muscles, the **platysma (C)**, the **buccinator (D)**, and the **posterior belly of the digastric (E)**. Its parasympathetic fibers innervate the submaxillary, submandibular, and lacrimal glands.

[Color A and B different shades of the same color. Color C-E different shades of red.]

The cell bodies of the sensory fibers that relay taste lie in the **geniculate ganglion (F)**, which is located in the petrous part of the temporal bone. Axons leaving the geniculate ganglion travel to the pons as a part of the nervus intermedius, and then synapse with other taste fibers in the **nucleus of the solitary tract (G)** (the upper portion of this nucleus is the sensory nucleus of the facial nerve). The efferent fibers then cross the midline and ascend to the ventral posteromedial (VPM) nucleus of the thalamus on the opposite side; from here the fibers travel through the internal capsule to the somatosensory cortex (Brodmann's areas 3,1,2; the postcentral gyrus).

The **motor root of the facial nerve (H)** arises from the **motor nucleus of the facial nerve (I)**, which is located in the posterolateral tegmentum of the pons, lateral to the abducens nucleus. Axons leaving this nucleus travel in a circle around the abducens nucleus and then pass to the pons, surfacing medial to the vestibulocochlear nerve.

The sensory and motor roots combined make up the facial nerve. The facial nerve arises from the pons and, with the cochlear nerve, enters the **internal acoustic meatus (J)**. From this point, it passes into the inner ear via the facial canal and forms the geniculate ganglion. The facial nerve then travels behind the pyramid, exits the skull through the stylomastoid foramen, and passes through the parotid gland to give off 5 branches that supply its effector muscles.

The parasympathetic fibers of the facial nerve arise from the **superior salivatory nucleus (K)**. These fibers join the motor fibers in supplying the muscles of facial expression and arise from the pons to innervate the submaxillary, submandibular, and lacrimal glands.

[Color G, H, I, and K different shades of similar colors.]

Clinical Correlates: *A well-known disorder involving the facial nerve is Bell's palsy. In Bell's palsy, patients experience weakness of both upper and lower facial muscles. Depending on the site of facial nerve damage, patients may also experience other problems, such as a decrease in lacrimation and taste sensation. The cause of this condition is unknown.*

○ Facial nerve	A	○ Posterior belly of the digastric	E	○ Motor nucleus of the facial nerve	I
○ Nervus intermedius	B	○ Geniculate ganglion	F	○ Internal acoustic meatus	J
○ Platysma	C	○ Nucleus of the solitary tract	G	○ Superior salivatory nucleus	K
○ Buccinator	D	○ Motor root of the facial nerve	H		

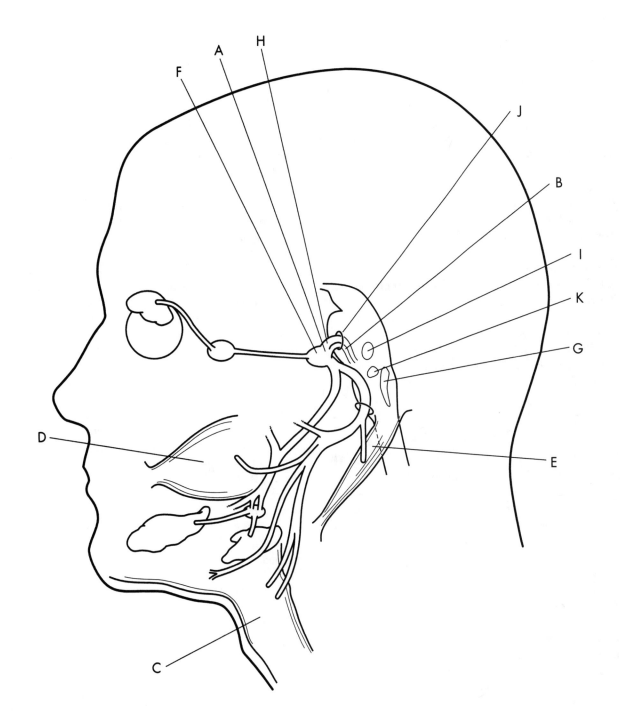

The Facial Nerve: CN VII

Chapter 4-11: CN VIII: Cochlear Portion and Auditory System

The vestibulocochlear nerve, not surprisingly, contains vestibular and cochlear portions. The cochlear portion, which is involved in hearing, will be discussed here along with the auditory system. The **cochlea (A)** of the inner ear is embedded in the petrous part of the temporal bone, and consists of three fluid-filled tubes coiled into roughly 2 1/2 turns (it resembles a snail) all the way to its apex; the helicotrema. The three tubes are the **scala vestibuli (B)**, the **scala media (C)**, and the **scala tympani (D)**. The first two are separated by Reissner's membrane; the latter two are separated by the **basement membrane (E)**. The scala vestibuli ends at the **oval window (F)** (at the base of the cochlea), and contains a fluid known as perilymph, which is similar in composition to cerebrospinal fluid; the scala tympani ends at the **round window (G)**, and is also filled with perilymph. The scala media is filled with a fluid known as endolymph, which contains a high concentration of potassium and a low concentration of sodium.

[Color B, C, and D different shades of the same color; do the same for F and G.]

The basilar membrane harbors the **organ of Corti (H)**, which is located in the cochlear duct and contains one row of motion-sensitive, inner and three rows of motion-sensitive, outer hair cells. These hair cells are essentially auditory receptors that generate action potentials in response to sound vibrations that move the basilar membrane. From the base of the cochlea, travelling to the helicotrema, the length of the hair cells progressively increase while the diameter of the hair cells decrease. This arrangement modulates the frequency at which the hair cells vibrate; the ones at the base vibrate at high frequency, and these vibrations are transmitted by the stapes of the middle ear to the scala vestibuli at the oval window, where the stapes is connected. Sound vibrations produce movement of the stapes; inward movement moves the fluid into the scala vestibuli and media, and outward movement moves the fluid out.

The bases of the hair cells are embedded in a web of nerve endings in the **cochlear portion of the vestibulocochlear nerve (I)**. The cell bodies of the acoustic nerve are located in the **spiral ganglion (J)** of the **modiolus (K)** (the bony segment around which the cochlea coils itself). These fibers then travel to the brain stem and synapse in the anterior and posterior cochlear nuclei in the upper medulla. From here, fibers of the cochlear nuclei travel to the inferior colliculus through several different pathways. Some axons cross to the other side of the brain stem to the superior olivary nucleus, while others travel to the superior olivary nucleus of the same side; many fibers then travel up the lateral lemniscus to the inferior colliculus. From the inferior colliculus the fibers travel to and synapse in the medial geniculate nucleus, and then extend to the auditory cortex in the superior temporal gyrus.

[Color K a light color.]

Therefore, sound waves travel across the **tympanic membrane (L)** (eardrum) of the outer ear into the middle ear. Here the ossicles of the middle ear, **incus (M)**, **malleus (N)**, and **stapes (O)**, transmit and amplify sound waves; the footplate of the stapes shoots the sound waves across the oval window into the scala vestibuli's perilymph. Movement of the perilymph produces waves of fluid that cause vibration of the basilar membrane. This stimulates the hair cells, producing nerve impulses that are first transmitted to the spiral ganglion and then travel to the auditory cortex in the superior temporal gyrus.

[Color M, N, and O different shades of the same color.]

Clinical Correlates: *Lesions of the cochlear portion of the vestibulocochlear nerve result in deafness.*

○ Cochlea	A	○ Oval window	F	○ Spiral ganglion	J
○ Scala vestibuli	B	○ Round window	G	○ Modiolus	K
○ Scala media	C	○ Organ of Corti	H	○ Tympanic membrane	L
○ Scala tympani	D	○ Cochlear portion of the vestibulocochlear nerve	I	○ Incus	M
○ Basement membrane	E			○ Malleus	N
				○ Stapes	O

The labyrinthine and cochlear apparatus, rotated down

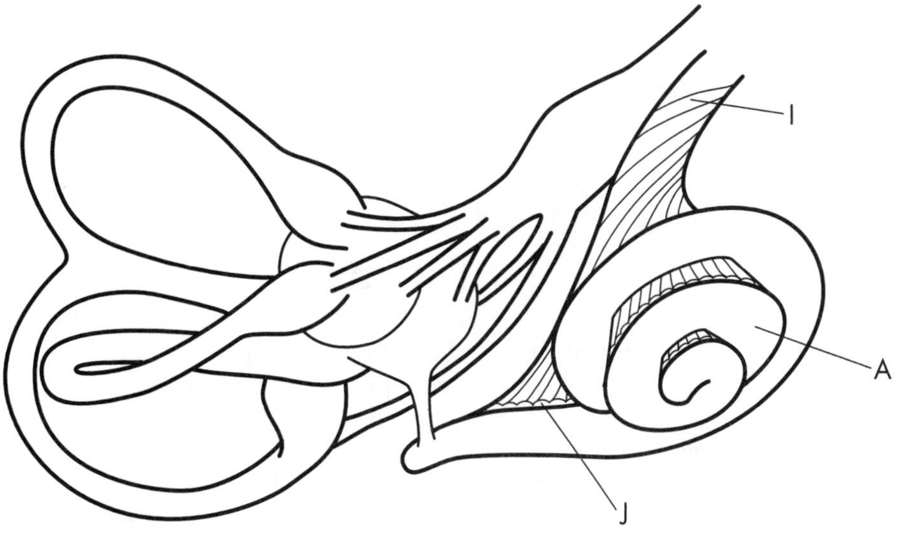

I

A

J

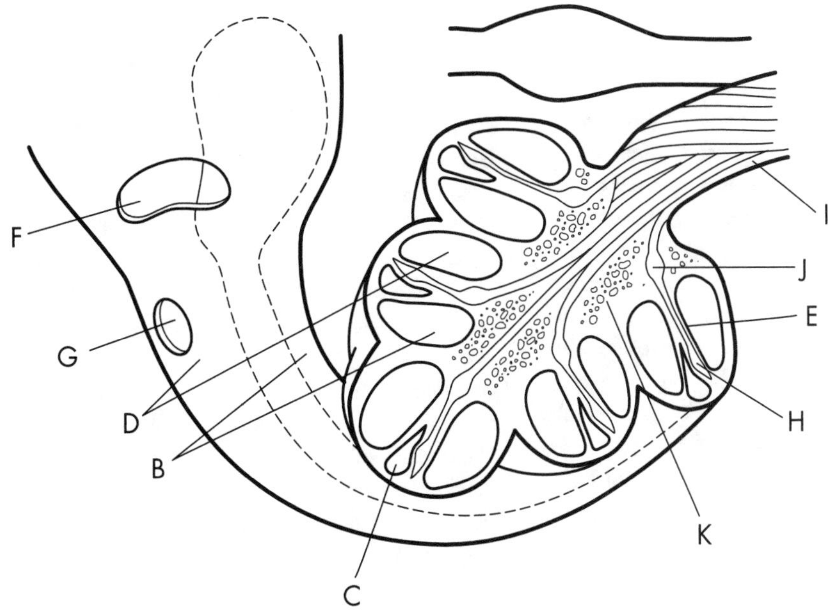

Section through the cochlea

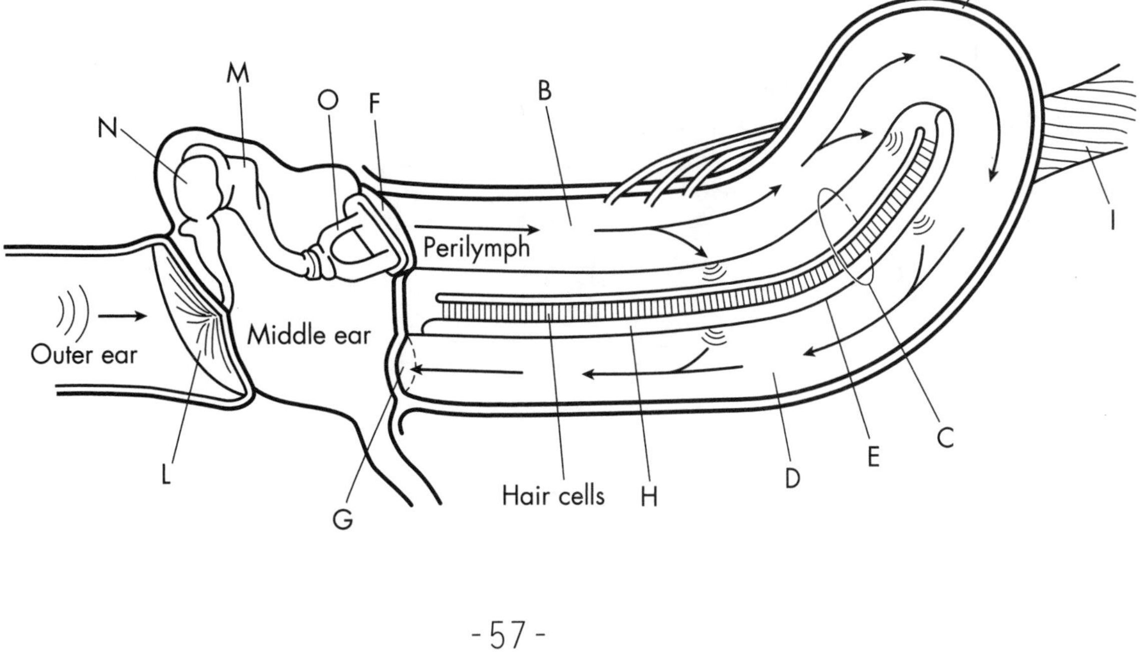

F

G

D

B

C

I

J

E

H

K

M

N

O

F

B

A

Perilymph

Outer ear

Middle ear

Hair cells

L

G

H

D

E

C

I

Chapter 4-12: CN VIII: Vestibular Portion and Balance

The vestibulocochlear nerve is a sensory nerve that consists of two portions; the **vestibular portion of vestibulocochlear nerve (A)** and the **cochlear portion of vestibulocochlear nerve (B)**. The vestibular portion relays information about equilibrium and balance from the inner ear, and the cochlear portion conveys sound information from the cochlea of the inner ear. The vestibular and cochlear portions are attached to the brain stem; they travel together to the **internal acoustic meatus (C)** and then diverge and continue to different portions of the inner ear.

[Color A and B different shades of the same color.]

The vestibular apparatus of the inner ear is involved with spacial orientation and equilibrium. It is composed of the **anterior semicircular canal (D)**, the **posterior semicircular canal (E)**, the **lateral semicircular canal (F)**, the **utricle (G)**, and the **saccule (H)**. The three semicircular canals are located at approximately right angles to each other, in the three planes of space. The walls of both the utricle and saccule contain a thickened area called the **macula (I)**, which is involved with linear acceleration. Each semicircular canal opens up at one of its ends; this area is called the ampulla, and inside is an elevated area called the **crista ampullaris (J)**. Each crista contains **hair cells (K)** that represent the vestibular receptor. **Cilia (L)** from the hair cells project into an overlying gelatinous structure known as the **cupula (M)**.

[Color D, E, and F different shades of the same color.]

Movement of the head pushes the endolymph of the semicircular canals into the ampulla, bending the cupula in the ampulla to one side. Bending of the cupula produces an action potential, which travels to the vestibular portion of the vestibulocochlear nerve and then on to the vestibular nuclei in the pons and medulla. Note that bending the cupula in one direction produces depolarization, while bending in the other direction produces hyperpolarization.

The macula, which are, as you may recall, raised areas within the utricle and saccule, are actually a group of receptors that respond to linear acceleration, that is, to the position of the head in relation to the ground; static equilibrium. The maculae harbor **macular hair cells (N)** and **macular supporting cells (O)**. The hair cells contain both **stereocilia (P)**, which are microvilli, and one **kinocilium (Q)**, which is a cilium. Overlying the hair cells is a gelatinous structure called the **otolithic membrane (R)**, and overlying this membrane are the **otoliths (S)**. Tilting the head causes the otolithic membrane to move, and this distorts the hair cells, triggering an action potential that travels down the vestibular portion of cranial nerve VIII.

Nerve fibers of the vestibular portion of the vestibulocochlear nerve arise from the **vestibular ganglion (T)** in the internal acoustic meatus. The vestibular ganglion separates into superior and inferior segments, and the peripheral processes of each division meet the hair cell receptors of the semicircular canals, utricle, and saccule. The nerve fibers then enter the brain stem at the cerebellopontine angle and travel to the vestibular nuclei; other fibers pass to the ipsilateral (same side) half of the cerebellum via the juxtarestiform body. Most of the vestibular fibers terminate in the vestibular nuclei (superior, inferior, lateral, medial), which lies in the floor of the fourth ventricle.

Clinical Correlates: *Lesions of the vestibular portion of the vestibulocochlear nerve upset one's balance. This phenomenon is known as vertigo.*

○ Vestibular portion of vestibulocochlear nerve A	○ Lateral semicircular canal F	○ Macular hair cells N
○ Cochlear portion of vestibulocochlear nerve B	○ Utricle G	○ Macular supporting cells O
○ Internal acoustic meatus C	○ Saccule H	○ Stereocilia P
○ Anterior semicircular canal D	○ Macula I	○ Kinocilium Q
○ Posterior semicircular canal E	○ Crista ampullaris J	○ Otolithic membrane R
	○ Hair cells K	○ Otoliths S
	○ Cilia L	○ Vestibular ganglion T
	○ Cupula M	

Membranous labyrinth

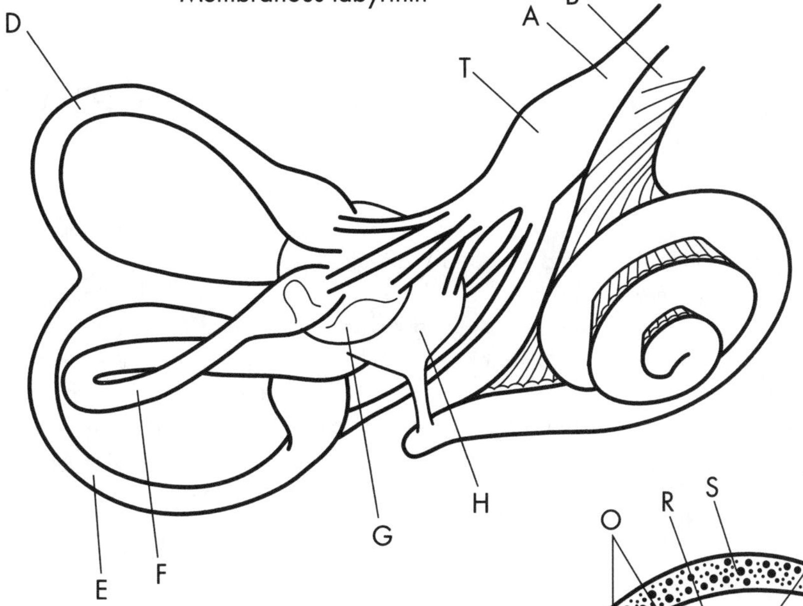

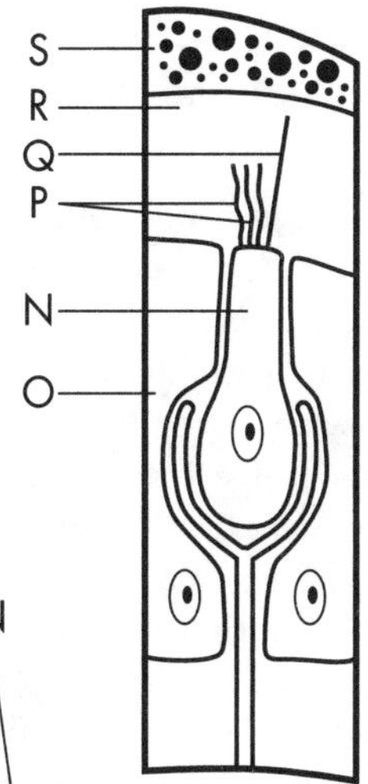

Details of a hair cell

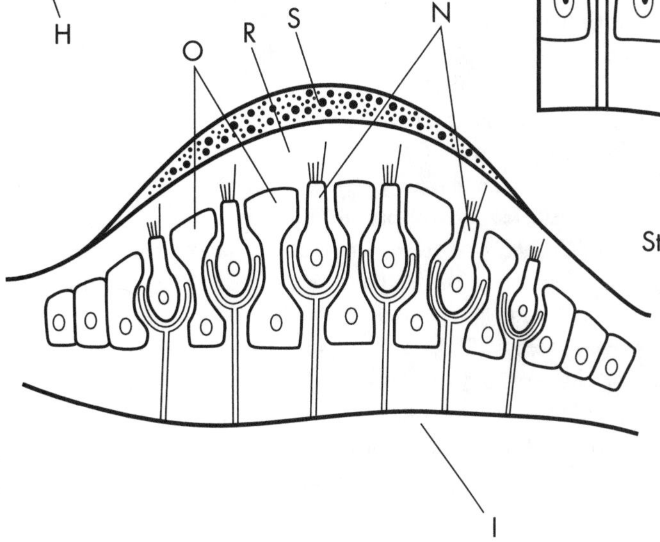

Structure of the macula

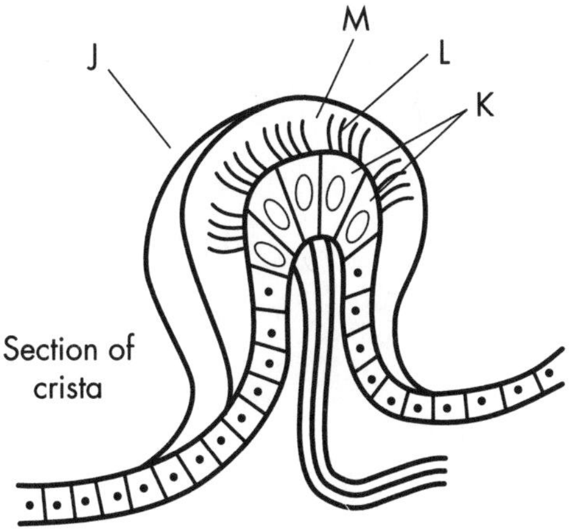

Section of crista

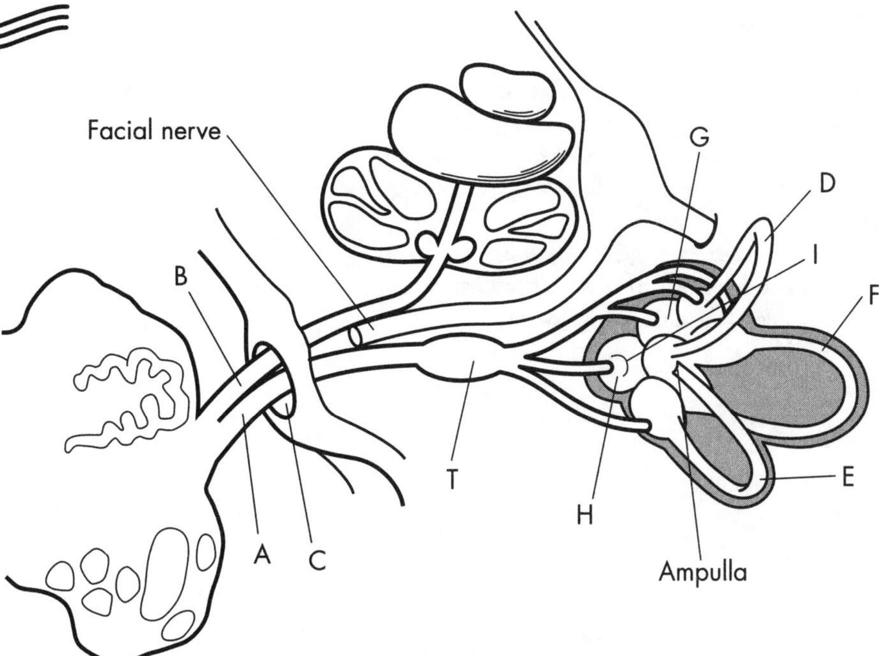

The vestibulocochlear (VIII) nerve

Facial nerve

Ampulla

Chapter 4-13: CN IX: Glossopharyngeal Nerve

The **glossopharyngeal nerve (A)** is made up of both sensory and motor fibers. The sensory fibers transmit taste information from the posterior third of the tongue; they also provide sensory innervation to the carotid body, carotid sinus, pharynx, tongue, and eustachian tube. The motor fibers supply the stylopharyngeus muscle. The parasympathetic fibers of the glossopharyngeal nerve innervate the **parotid gland (B)**.

The sensory fibers of the glossopharyngeal nerve emerge from three sites: (1) the General Visceral Afferent (GVA) fibers, (2) the General Somatic Afferent (GSA) fibers, and (3) the Specific Visceral Afferent (SVA) fibers. The GVA fibers carry sensations from the pharynx; the GSA fibers carry sensory information from the skin behind the ear, and the SVA fibers carry taste information from the posterior third of the tongue. The cell bodies of the GSA lie in the **superior ganglion of the glossopharyngeal nerve (C)**, and their axons terminate in the **spinal nucleus of the trigeminal nerve (D)**. The cell bodies of both the GVA and SVA lie in the **inferior ganglion of the glossopharyngeal nerve (E)**, and their axons terminate in the **nucleus of the solitary tract (F)**. Nerve fibers cross the median and travel to the opposite thalamic nuclei, and from there their axons traverse the internal capsule to reach the somatosensory cortex (Brodmann's areas 3,1,2; the postcentral gyrus).

[Color C and E different shades of the same color.]

The motor fibers of the glossopharyngeal nerve function in the following ways: The Somatic Visceral Efferents (SVE) fibers, which supply the stylopharyngeus muscle, arise from the **nucleus ambiguus (G)**. As you will see, in fact, the SVE fibers of cranial nerves IX, X, and XI all arise from the nucleus ambiguus.

The parasympathetic fibers, or the General Visceral Efferent (GVE) fibers, arise from the **inferior salivatory nucleus (H)**; these fibers terminate in the **otic ganglion (I)**.

Glossopharyngeal nerve rootlets leave the upper medulla and join to form the glossopharyngeal nerve. At this point they pass, along with the vagus nerve, through the jugular foramen; the sensory ganglia (both superior and inferior) are located within this foramen. From here, the nerve passes between the internal jugular vein and internal carotid artery and supplies and travels along the posterior margin of the stylopharyngeus muscle in its journey to the base of the tongue, where it divides into branches and supplies the tongue's effector muscles.

[Color D, F, G, and H different shades of the same (or similar) color.]

Clinical Correlates: *Lesions involving the glossopharyngeal nerve result in symptoms such as a loss of sensations from the pharynx, loss of the gag reflex, and loss of taste from the posterior third of the tongue.*

○ Glossopharyngeal nerve	A	○ Spinal nucleus of the trigeminal nerve	D	○ Nucleus ambiguus	G
○ Parotid gland	B	○ Inferior ganglion of the glossopharyngeal nerve	E	○ Inferior salivatory nucleus	H
○ Superior ganglion of the glossopharyngeal nerve	C	○ Nucleus of the solitary tract	F	○ Otic ganglion	I

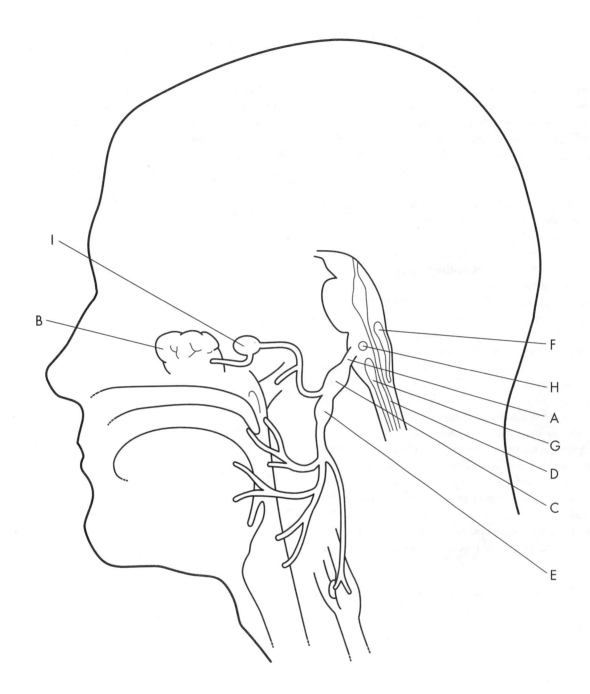

The glossopharyngeal nerve

CHAPTER FOUR

Chapter 4-14: CN X: Vagus Nerve

The **vagus nerve (A)** carries both motor and sensory nerve fibers. The motor fibers innervate the viscera of the neck, thorax, and abdomen; they innervate striated muscles of the soft palate, pharynx, larynx, and uvula. The sensory fibers innervate the larynx and pharynx, as well as the external acoustic meatus, the tympanic membrane, and the thoracic and abdominal viscera. In addition, sensory fibers relay taste information from the epiglottis. The parasympathetic fibers of the vagus nerve innervate the neck viscera, thoracic viscera, and abdominal viscera up to the left colic flexure.

The motor fibers supplying the soft palate, larynx, and pharynx eminate from the **nucleus ambiguus (B)**, which is located deep in the reticular formation of the lateral medulla.

Most parasympathetic fibers arise from the **dorsal motor nucleus (C)** of the vagus, but the parasympathetic fibers that innervate the heart arise from the nucleus ambiguus.

The sensory fibers that relay information from thoracic and abdominal viscera have cell bodies that lie in the **inferior ganglion of the vagus nerve (D)** (also known as the nodose ganglion); the central processes of the inferior ganglion extend to the **nucleus of the solitary tract (E)**. The fibers that relay general sensory information from the external acoustic meatus and the tympanic membrane have their cell bodies in the **superior ganglion of the vagus nerve (F)** (also known as the jugular ganglion), and the central processes of the superior ganglion terminate in the **spinal nucleus of the trigeminal nerve (G)**. The sensory fibers that convey taste information from the epiglottis have their cell bodies in the inferior ganglion of the vagus nerve, and the central processes terminate in the nucleus of the solitary tract.

[Color B, C, E, and G different shades of the same (or similar) color; do the same for D and F.]

The vagus nerve exits the upper medulla from the postolivary sulcus in the form of rootlets that quickly join, and then exits the cranium, along with cranial nerves IX and XI, through the jugular foramen, where the superior and inferior vagal ganglia are found. The nerve descends in the neck within the carotid sheath along with the internal jugular vein, the common carotid artery, and the internal carotid artery.

Clinical Correlates: Lesions of the vagus nerve produce weakness of the pharyngeal and laryngeal muscles, loss of the cough reflex, and laryngeal anesthesia.

○ Vagus nerve   A   ○ Inferior ganglion of   ○ Superior ganglion of
                                             the vagus nerve   D   the vagus nerve   F
○ Nucleus ambiguus   B
                                         ○ Nucleus of the   ○ Spinal nucleus of
○ Dorsal motor nucleus   C   solitary tract   E   the trigeminal nerve   G

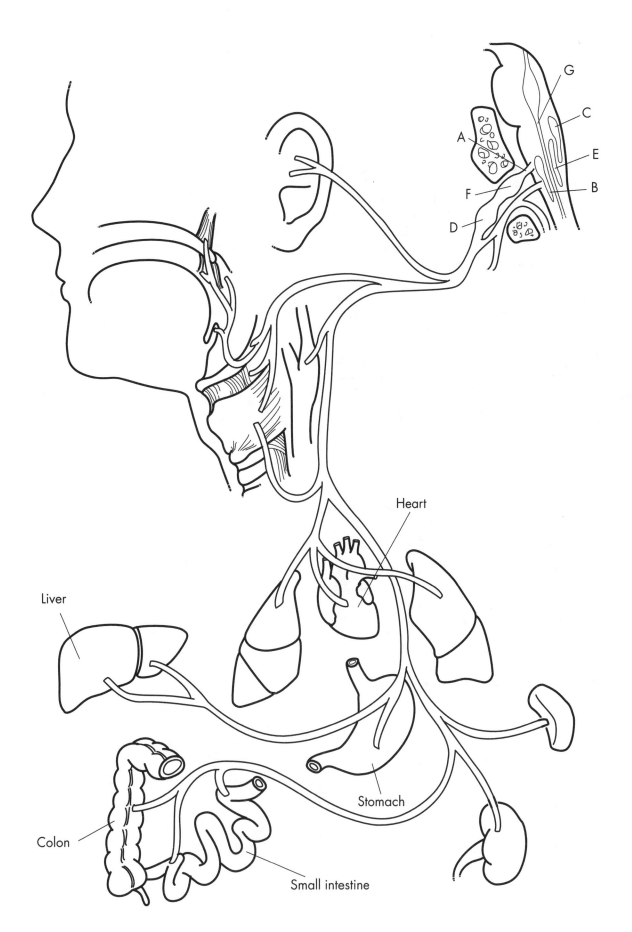

A

G

C

E

B

F

D

Heart

Liver

Stomach

Colon

Small intestine

Chapter 4-15: CN XI: Spinal Accessory Nerve

The **spinal accessory nerve (A)** is a motor nerve; it is called the spinal accessory nerve because it is formed from the joining of spinal and accessory roots; specifically the **spinal root (C)** and the (accessory) **cranial roots (B)**. The spinal root supplies the **trapezius muscle (D)** and **sternocleidomastoid muscle (E)**, and the cranial root supplies the laryngeal muscles (with the exception of the cricothyroid muscle) via the recurrent laryngeal nerve.

The spinal root begins as rootlets in the spinal nucleus, located in the anterior horn of cervical segments C1-C5 of the spinal cord. These spinal rootlets exit the spinal cord between the dorsal and ventral spinal nerve roots, and then join to form an ascending nerve trunk (the spinal root) behind the denticulate ligament. The spinal root then enters the skull via the **foramen magnum (F)**, where it unites with the cranial root. Both roots leave the skull through the jugular foramen, and go on to innervate their respective effector muscles.

[Color A, B, and C different shades of the same color. Color D and E different shades of red.]

The cranial (accessory) root is formed from nerve fibers originating in the **nucleus ambiguus (G)**. The accessory rootlets emerge from the subolivary portion of the medulla, along with the rootlets of the glossopharyngeal and vagus nerves. The accessory rootlets then join to form the accessory root, which then joins the spinal root to form the spinal accessory nerve. The spinal accessory nerve leaves the cranium through the jugular foramen, and here the roots separate; the cranial root joins the vagus nerve and provides the majority of the motor fibers of the pharyngeal and recurrent laryngeal segments of the vagus nerve.

Clinical Correlates: *Damage to the spinal accessory nerve results in weakness of the sternocleidomastoid muscle, which makes it difficult to turn one's head to the opposite side. It also causes weakness of the trapezius muscle, which makes it difficult to raise the shoulders (in a shrug). These difficulties would occur on the side where the lesion occurred if the spinal accessory nerve itself was damaged.*

○	Spinal accessory nerve	A	○ Spinal root	C	○ Foramen magnum F
○	Cranial roots	B	○ Trapezius muscle	D	○ Nucleus ambiguus G
			○ Sternocleidomastoid muscle	E	

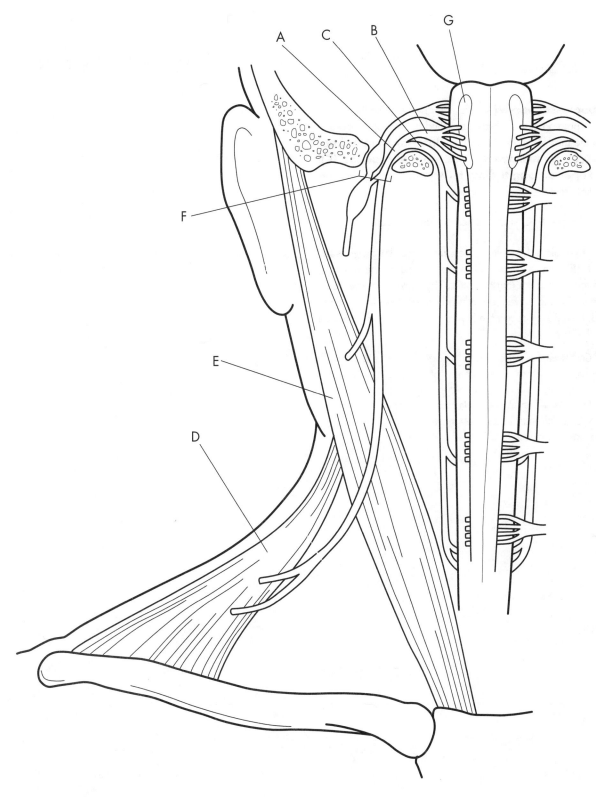

The spinal accessory nerve

Chapter 4-16: CN XII: Hypoglossal Nerve

The **hypoglossal nerve (A)** is a motor nerve. With the exception of the palatoglossus, which is supplied by the vagus nerve, it supplies the muscles of the tongue: the **inferior longitudinal muscle (B)**, the **transverse and vertical muscles (C)**, and the **superior longitudinal muscle (D)**. The tongue muscles mediate movement of the tongue.

[Color B, C, and D different shades of red.]

The hypoglossal nerve arises from the **hypoglossal nucleus (E)**, which is located in the midline of the medulla, beneath the floor of the fourth ventricle. Hypoglossal nerve fibers travel ventrally and leave the medulla between the olive and the pyramid, then pass through the hypoglossal canal and innervate the muscles of the tongue.

Clinical Correlates: *Damage to the hypoglossal nerve or the hypoglossal nucleus produce weakness of the tongue, fasciculations of the tongue, and deviation of the tongue, of and to the same side of the lesion. More central lesions (above the level of the hypoglossal nucleus) cause the tongue to deviate to the opposite side of the lesion.*

○ Hypoglossal nerve   A   ○ Transverse and vertical muscles   C   ○ Superior longitudinal muscles   D

○ Inferior longitudinal muscle   B   ○ Hypoglossal nucleus   E

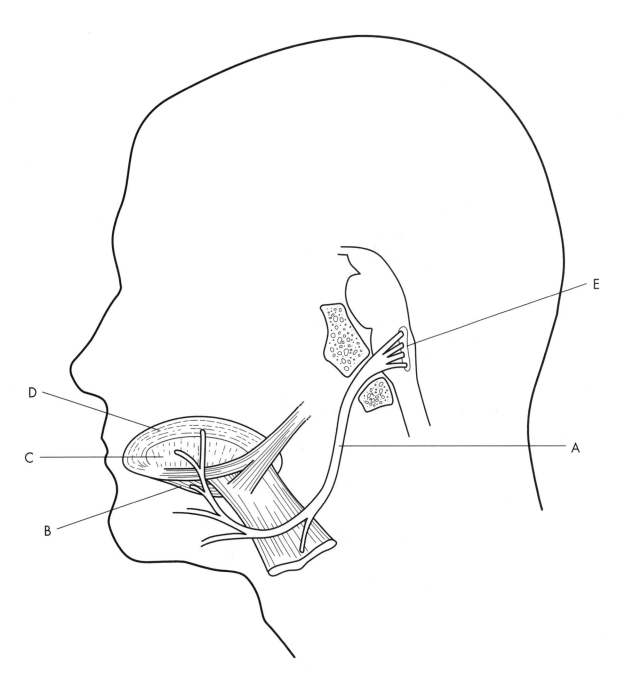

The hypoglossal (XII) nerve

THE CRANIAL NERVES
self assessment

A. Olfactory nerve
B. Optic nerve
C. Oculomotor nerve
D. Trochlear nerve
E. Trigeminal nerve
F. Abducens nerve
G. Facial nerve
H. Vestibulocochlear nerve
I. Glossopharyngeal nerve
J. Vagus nerve
K. Spinal accessory nerve
L. Hypoglossal nerve

1. Moves eyes up, down, and up/lateral

2. Damage to this nerve causes Bell's palsy

3. Associated with the lateral geniculate body

4. Associated with the semicircular canals

5. Arises from semilunar ganglion

the ventricular system and cerebrospinal fluid circulation

Chapter 5-1: the Ventricular System and Cerebrospinal Fluid Circulation

The ventricular system of the brain consists of the following chambers: two **lateral ventricles (A)**, a **third ventricle (B)**, a **cerebral aqueduct (C)**, and a **fourth ventricle (D)**. The lateral ventricles both have three horns: the **anterior horn of the lateral ventricle (E)**, the **inferior horn of the lateral ventricle (F)**, and the **posterior horn of the lateral ventricle (G)**. The ventricular chambers communicate with one another via foramina: (1) the **interventricular foramen (H)** is the opening through which the two lateral ventricles communicate, (2) the **foramen of Magendie (I)** and the paired **foramen of Luschka (J)** allow communication between the ventricular system and the subarachnoid space, which is the compartment in which the cerebrospinal fluid circulates. It is important to understand that the accompanying diagram represents spaces, or cavities.

[Color E, F, and G different shades of the same color. Color the remaining structures different colors; make I and J different shades of the same color.]

The ventricles all have a lining called the ependyma that is made up of cuboidal cells. Cerebrospinal fluid (CSF) is an essentially non-cellular liquid with a makeup that is similar to that of plasma: It contains a fair amount of sodium chloride, as well as protein, glucose, and potassium. Its primary function is to act as a cushion for the brain, preventing it from becoming damaged in the cranial vault. When the head undergoes a sudden change in movement (as occurs in a sudden stop or acceleration), or when it gets hit, the effect of the blow of the brain against the cranial vault is dampened by the cerebrospinal fluid; the brain simply floats within it.

So how is CSF manufactured? Most of it is formed by the choroid plexus, which is a network of blood vessels located in the lateral, third, and fourth ventricles. It secretes the CSF from its cells through active transport at a rate of 500 ml/day; the volume of CSF in the brain is maintained between 90 and 150 ml. Since so much CSF is produced each day, it must be continually reabsorbed or its accumulation within the brain would result in intracranial pressure that would seriously damage the brain.

The pathway of CSF from the choroid plexus is as follows: CSF from the lateral and third ventricles travels down the cerebral aqueduct to the fourth ventricle, which also contributes some CSF; from here, the fluid enters the subarachnoid space (specifically, the cisterna magna) through the foramen of Magendie and the two foramina of Luschka; it then circulates through the cerebrum and passes into the dural venous sinuses (this is where much CSF is reabsorbed) through outpouchings of the arachnoid known as **arachnoid villi (K)**. The arachnoid villi act as one-way valves to help control the hydrostatic pressure. For instance, if the pressure in the venous system is greater than the pressure in the CSF system, the villi remain closed, and if the CSF pressure is higher than the dural venous pressure, they open.

Clinical Correlates: *A condition known as hydrocephalus occurs when there is a blockage in the circulation or reabsorption of CSF. Since the rate of CSF formation remains fairly constant, a blockage in flow results in the accumulation of CSF within the cranial vault and progressive dilation of the ventricles. There are 2 main types of hydrocephalus: Communicating hydrocephalus and non-communicating hydrocephalus. Communication refers to whether or not the blockage allows the ventricles to communicate with the subarachnoid space. In communicating hydrocephalus, the blockage occurs outside of the ventricular chambers and the CSF is not inhibited from entering the subarachnoid space, while in non-communicating hydrocephalus the blockage lies within the ventricular chambers themselves; this blockade prevents the ventricles from communicating with the subarachnoid space.*

○ Lateral ventricles   A

○ Third ventricle   B

○ Cerebral aqueduct   C

○ Fourth ventricle   D

○ Anterior horn of the lateral ventricle   E

○ Inferior horn of the lateral ventricle   F

○ Posterior horn of the lateral ventricle   G

○ Interventricular foramen   H

○ Foramen of Magendie   I

○ Foramen of Luschka   J

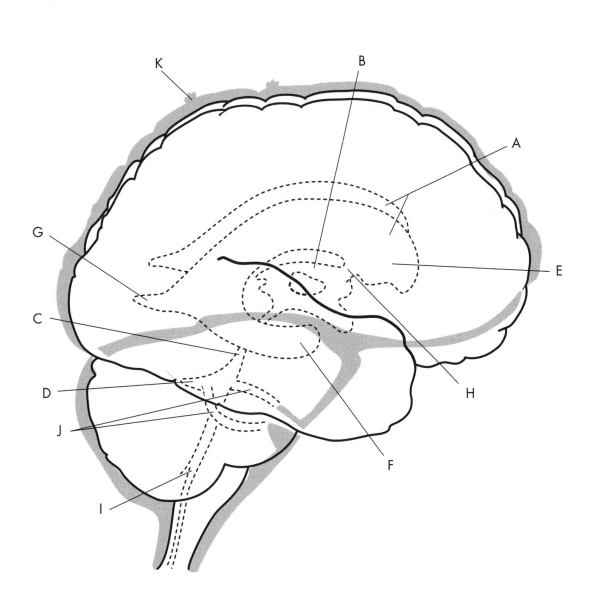

Path of cerebrospinal fluid flow

A. Inferior horn of lateral ventricle
B. Anterior horn of lateral ventricle
C. Interventricular foramen
D. Ependyma
E. Arachnoid villi
F. Foramen of Magendie
G. Choroid plexus
H. Communicating hydrocephalus
I. Posterior horn of lateral ventricle
J. Noncommunicating hydrocephalus
K. Cerebral aqueduct

1. Site of cerebrospinal fluid production

2. Cerebrospinal fluid is reabsorbed through this structure

3. This condition would result from blockage of the foramina of Luschka and Magendie

4. Allows communication between the lateral ventricles

5. Lining of ventricles

the limbic system

Chapter 6-1: The Limbic System

The limbic system is involved with emotion, memory, motivation, behavior, and autonomic function. It is composed of a group of structures that are primarily located on the medial aspect of the cerebral hemisphere. The components of the limbic system are as follows: the **parahippocampal gyrus (A)**, the **uncus (B)**, the **subcallosal gyrus (C)**, the **cingulate gyrus (D)**, the **orbitofrontal cortex (E)**, the **hippocampus (F)**, the **amygdaloid body (G)**, the **parolfactory area (H)**, the **anterior nucleus of the thalamus (I)**, the **mammillary bodies (J)**, and the hypothalamus.

[Color A-K different colors.]

Memory and learning are functions of the hippocampus. The output pathway for the hippocampus is the fornix, and roughly half of the fibers of the fornix terminate in the mammillary bodies. The mamillary bodies then project to the anterior nuclei of the thalamus via the **mammillothalamic tract (K)**, and the anterior nuclei project to the cingulate gyrus. The Papez circuit is a pathway for memory that travels from the hippocampal formation, to the hypothalamus, and on to the cingulate gyrus.

The amygdala is involved in providing emotion and autonomic responses, but it also receives a small amount of olfactory input. When the amygdala is stimulated, the emotion of rage and the desire to fight are produced. The amygdala receives input from the sensory cortex and projects to the basal ganglia, the thalamus, the hypothalamus, the hippocampus, and the brain stem.

The limbic cortex, which is made up of the cingulate gyrus, the parahippocampal gyrus, and the hippocampal formation, is involved with learning and briefly stores memory; destruction of the circuitry of the limbic cortex results in a loss of the ability to learn new information.

Clinical Correlates: *An example of an emotional disturbance that results from damage to one of the limbic structures is the Klüver-Bucy syndrome. It is caused by a bilateral destruction of the amygdala. The person loses the capacity for fear, becomes hypersexual and less aggressive, and quickly forgets things.*

○ Parahippocampal gyrus	A	○ Orbitofrontal cortex	E	○ Anterior nucleus of the thalamus	I
○ Uncus	B	○ Hippocampus	F	○ Mammillary bodies	J
○ Subcallosal gyrus	C	○ Amygdaloid body	G	○ Mammillothalamic tract	K
○ Cingulate gyrus	D	○ Parolfactory area	H		

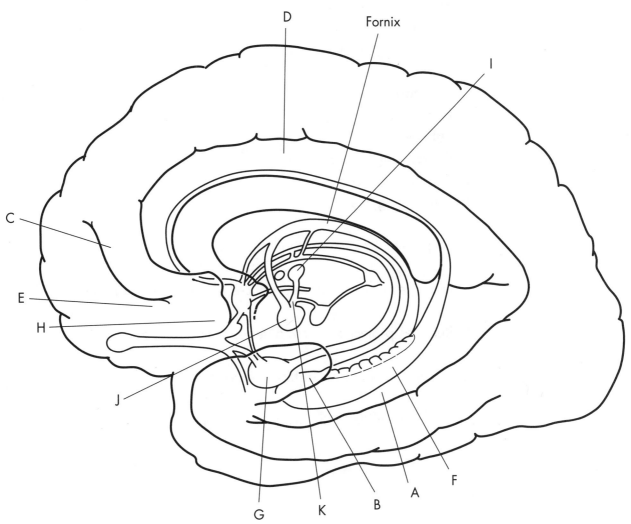

D

Fornix

I

C

E

H

J

G

K

B

A

F

Anatomy of the limbic system

THE LIMBIC SYSYEM

self assessment

A. Parahippocampal gyrus
B. Fornix
C. Mammillary body
D. Uncus
E. Amygdala
F. Hypothalamus
G. Subcallosal gyrus
H. Orbitofrontal cortex
I. Parolfactory area
J. Cingulate gyrus

1. Projects to the anterior thalamic nuclei

2. Damage to this structure produces Klüver-Bucy syndrome

3. Receives projections from anterior thalamic nuclei

4. Carries output fibers of hippocampus

5. Involved with fight/flight, rage reactions

7

CHAPTER SEVEN

the thalamic complex

Chapter 7-1: Thalamus: Anatomy and Nuclei

The thalamus is composed primarily of gray matter and is located in each of the two cerebral hemispheres. It is made up of the dorsal thalamus, the hypothalamus, the epithalamus, and the subthalamus; together, these make up the diencephalon.

A thalamus is located on either side of the third ventricle, and from there it extends laterally to the medial border of the **posterior limb of the internal capsule (A)**. The two thalami are connected by a band of gray matter that crosses the third ventricle, known as the **interthalamic adhesion (B)** (also called the massa intermedia). The thalamus is an egg-shaped structure that lies with its pointed end facing anteriorly. Anterior to posterior it extends from the intraventricular foramen of Monro to the posterior commissure (not shown); superior to inferior it extends from the roof of the third ventricle to the hypothalamic sulcus, which is a superficial crease on the lateral wall of the third ventricle that separates the thalamus from the hypothalamus. The medial surface of the thalamus forms a portion of the lateral wall of the third ventricle, and the structure is covered by thin layers of white matter on its superior and lateral surfaces: the layer on the superior surface of the thalamus is called the **stratum zonale (C)**, and the layer covering the lateral surface is called the **external medullary lamina (D)**.

The thalamus is divided into anterior, lateral, and medial segments by a thin plate of white matter that contains nerve fibers that travel from one thalamic nucleus to another; this plate is known as the **internal medullary lamina (E)**. The internal medullary lamina is a Y-shaped structure that divides the thalamus such that the **anterior nuclei (F)** of the thalamus lie between the two forks of the Y and the lateral and medial nuclei lie on either side of the stalk of the Y. Some thalamic nuclei also lie *within* the internal medullary lamina, the largest of which is the centromedian nucleus. The **reticular nucleus (G)** overlies the lateral surface of the thalamus and separates the external medullary lamina from the posterior limb of the internal capsule. The thalamic nuclei are named according to their location.

The thalamic nuclei can be divided into groups if we use the internal medullary lamina as the reference point. Lateral to the internal medullary lamina are two groups of nuclei; one group lies below the other. Let us call the more dorsal of the two groups the lateral group, and the more ventral, the ventral group. The lateral group consists of the following nuclei: lateral dorsal (LD), lateral posterior (LP), and pulvinar. The ventral group consists of the following nuclei: ventral anterior (VA), ventral lateral (VL), ventral posterolateral (VPL), and ventral posteromedial (VPM). The medial side of the internal medullary lamina harbors the medial dorsal (MD) nucleus. The anterior-most part of thalamus harbors the anterior nuclei (AN), and the posterior-most part is formed by the pulvinar, which is the largest of the thalamic nuclear masses. Finally we have the two nuclei that lie in the ventral and posterior portion of the thalamus and are overshadowed by the pulvinar; these are known as the lateral geniculate body (LGB) and the medial geniculate body (MGB). The significance of these nuclei is indicated by the areas of the brain that they project to, which will be discussed next.

[Color the nuclei of each group different shades of the same (or similar) color.]

○ Posterior limb of the internal capsule **A**	○ Stratum zonale **C**	○ Internal medullary lamina **E**
○ Interthalamic adhesion **B**	○ External medullary lamina **D**	○ Anterior nuclei **F**
		○ Reticular nuclei **G**

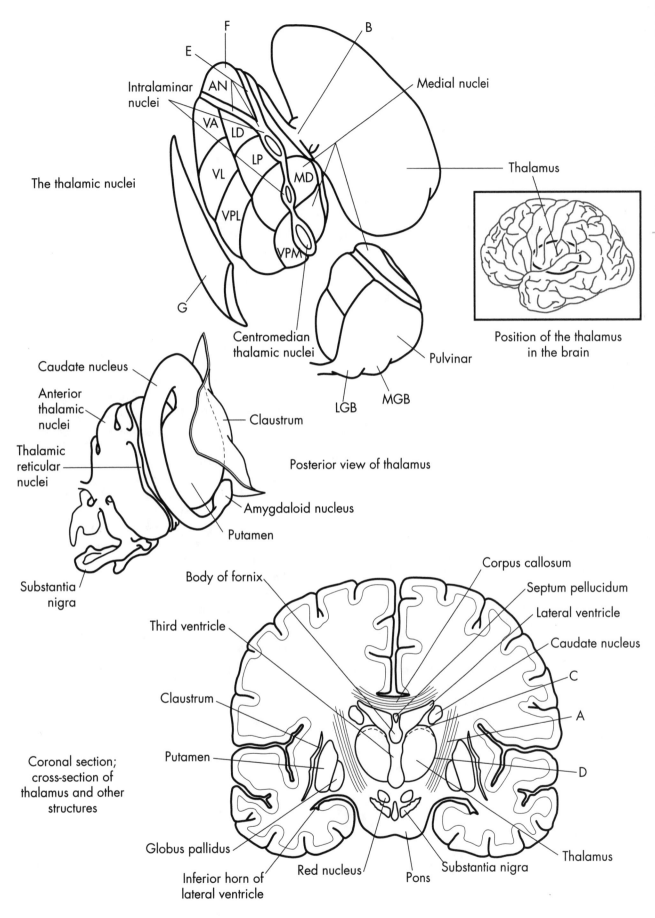

The thalamic nuclei

F
E
Intralaminar nuclei
AN
VA
LD
LP
VL
MD
VPL
VPM
G
Centromedian thalamic nuclei

B
Medial nuclei

Thalamus

Pulvinar

LGB   MGB

Position of the thalamus in the brain

Caudate nucleus

Anterior thalamic nuclei

Thalamic reticular nuclei

Claustrum

Posterior view of thalamus

Amygdaloid nucleus

Putamen

Substantia nigra

Body of fornix

Corpus callosum

Septum pellucidum

Lateral ventricle

Caudate nucleus

Third ventricle

C

A

Claustrum

Coronal section; cross-section of thalamus and other structures

Putamen

D

Globus pallidus

Inferior horn of lateral ventricle

Red nucleus

Pons

Substantia nigra

Thalamus

Chapter 7-2: Thalamus: Connections

The thalamus is the principal gateway for all sensory input, with the exception of smell. Sensory input to the cerebral cortex comes from the brainstem, the spinal cord, the cerebellum, and parts of the cerebrum. The thalamus is so important to the cerebral cortex that almost every area of the cerebral cortex has its own satellite center in the thalamus. As a result, exciting one specific region of the thalamus results in the activation of a corresponding specific region in the cerebral cortex. It is important to note that the communication between the thalamus and the cerebral cortex is bidirectional; the thalamus send signals to the cerebral cortex, and the cerebral cortex sends signals back to the thalamus.

The majority of the thalamic nuclei project to the cerebral cortex, but the thalamic connections with the basal ganglia will be discussed in the basal ganglia chapter.

[Use the same color for all the projections of each structure.]

The precise neuronal circuitry of the lateral group remains unclear, but it is believed to have connections with other groups within the thalamus in addition to its connections to the cerebral cortex. The LD nucleus has connections with the inferior parietal and posterior cingulate cortex, the LP connects with a large portion of the parietal cortex, and the pulvinar connects with much of the temporal, parietal, and occipital cortex.

In the ventral group, the VA receives signals from the **globus pallidus (A)** and **substantia nigra (B)**. The fibers from the globus pallidus reach the VA in the form of two tracts; the **ansa lenticularis (C)** and the **lenticular fasciculus (D)**; these fibers are called pallidothalamic fibers; the name signifies that they come from the pallidus and travel to the thalamus. Fibers known as nigrothalamic fibers arise from the **pars compacta (E)** of the substantia nigra and then enter the VA. The mammillothalamic tract also passes through the VA, and the VA projects to the premotor cortex. The VL receives input from the cerebellum as well as the globus pallidus and the substantia nigra, and it projects to the primary motor cortex. The VPL receives the sensory tracts, known as the medial lemniscus, and

the spinothalamic tracts (discussed later), and the VPM receives the trigeminal and gustatory tracts. The VPL is the end site of two sensory tracts; the spinothalamic tract and the medial lemniscus (discussed later). The VPL and VPM both project to the somatosensory cortex via the posterior limb of the internal capsule.

The AN and MD are both associated with the limbic system, which is a system that is involved with emotions, behavior, and memory. The AN receives the mammillothalamic tract, which carries signals from the hippocampus and projects to the cingulate gyrus (via the anterior limb of the internal capsule) and the limbic cortex. The MD receives input from the hypothalamus, the substantia nigra, and the amygdala; it projects to the prefrontal cortex. The CM receives input from the globus pallidus, and projects to the striatum, rather than the cerebral cortex.

The reticular nucleus is a thin sheet of neurons that covers the lateral aspect of the thalamus and separates the external medullary lamina from the posterior limb of the internal capsule. It receives input from the reticular formation (of the brainstem), the globus pallidus, and the entire cerebral cortex, and it projects primarily to other thalamic nuclei.

The MGB and LGB are collectively termed the metathalamus. The MGB is also known as the auditory relay nucleus and it receives input from the brachium of the inferior colliculus, which is a structure involved with the auditory system. The MGB projects to the auditory cortex of the temporal lobe. The LGB is known as a visual relay nucleus and receives input from the optic tract; it projects to the visual cortex, which is located in the occipital lobe.

Clinical Correlates: *Lesions of different portions of the thalamic system produce different effects. Lesions of the subthalamus often produce hemiballismus (see plate 8.2). A lesion of the thalamus (specifically, the VPL) often causes a loss of sensation, most commonly position sense, on the contralateral side of the body.*

○ Globus pallidus	A	○ Ansa lenticularis	C	○ Pars compacta	E
○ Substantia nigra	B	○ Lenticular fasciculus	D		

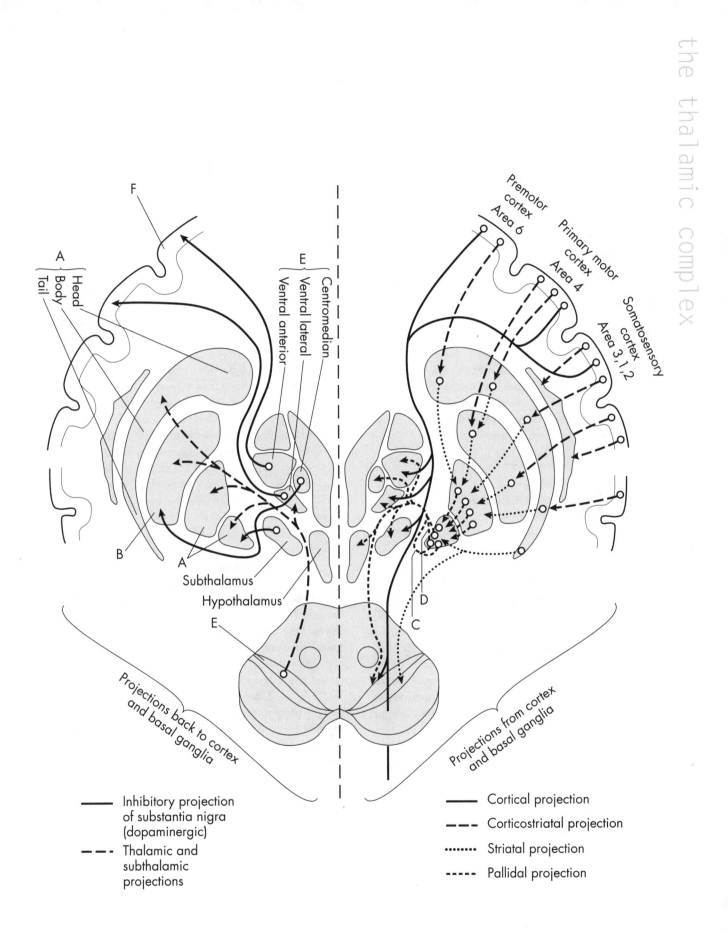

Premotor cortex Area 6
Primary motor cortex Area 4
Somatosensory cortex Area 3,1,2

F

A {Head Body Tail

E {Ventral lateral Ventral anterior

Centromedian

B

A

Subthalamus

Hypothalamus

E

D

C

Projections back to cortex and basal ganglia

Projections from cortex and basal ganglia

——— Inhibitory projection of substantia nigra (dopaminergic)

– – – Thalamic and subthalamic projections

——— Cortical projection

– – – Corticostriatal projection

· · · · · Striatal projection

- - - - Pallidal projection

Chapter 7-3: Hypothalamus: Anatomy and Nuclei

The hypothalamus, which forms the inferior-most region of the diencephalon, is located ventral to the thalamus and is separated from it by the **hypothalamic sulcus (A)**. Anterior to posterior, it extends from the **lamina terminalis (B)** to the **interpeduncular fossa (C)**. Its inferior boundary is formed by the **tuber cinereum (D)**. It forms the lateral and inferior walls of the third ventricle and, anterior to posterior, reaches from the **optic chiasm (E)** to the caudal margin of the **mamillary bodies (F)**. Its lateral border is formed by the internal capsule. Neighboring structures of the hypothalamus include: the optic chiasm, the pituitary gland, the **infundibulum (G)**, and the **fornix (H)**. Note that the pituitary gland has two parts: the **anterior pituitary (I)** and **posterior pituitary (I₁)**; these are also known as the adenohypophysis and neurohypophysis, respectively.

[Color I and I₁ different shades of the same color.]

The nuclei of the hypothalamus may be divided into three zones: the periventricular zone, the medial zone, and the lateral zone. The nuclei in each of the zones serve specified functions, which will be discussed later. The major nuclei will be mentioned here.

Moving in an anteroposterior direction, the nuclei of the periventricular zone include the following: part of the **preoptic nucleus (lateral) (J)**, the **suprachiasmatic nucleus (K)**, the **paraventricular nucleus (L)**, the **infundibular nucleus (M)**, and the **posterior nucleus (N)**. The nuclei of the medial zone, from anterior to posterior section, include the following nuclei: the medial preoptic nucleus, the **anterior nucleus (O)**, **dorsomedial nucleus (P)**, and the **ventromedial nucleus (Q)**. The lateral zone includes the following nuclei: part of the preoptic nucleus, and the **supraoptic nucleus (R)**. Note that the preoptic area is a part of all three zones.

[Color each of the nuclei a different color.]

The preoptic nuclei lie in the periventricular area, surrounding the third ventricle. The suprachiasmatic nucleus, as the name implies, lies just dorsal to the optic chiasm, and the paraventricular nucleus lies just beneath the ependyma (a membrane that lines the ventricles) of the third ventricle. The infundibular nucleus is located in the ventral-most portion of the third ventricle, while the posterior nucleus is located close to the mamillary bodies. The dorsomedial nucleus borders the third ventricle, and the supraoptic nucleus lies dorsal to the optic tract.

The hypothalamus plays a large role in the endocrine system; it modulates the release of hormones that are essential for the proper functioning of various organ systems. The hypothalamus serves its function through its association with the pituitary gland, and together they form what is called the hypophyseal portal system, which we will discuss in more detail later. Drives such as thirst and hunger are controlled by the hypothalamus, and this organ is also involved with the regulation of emotion and behavior; in this capacity it is associated with the limbic system. In addition, the hypothalamus is involved in the regulation of autonomic functions such as blood pressure and temperature regulation.

The nuclei of the periventricular zone are involved with control of the autonomic system, the neuroendocrine system, and biological rhythms, and the nuclei of the medial zone are involved primarily in homeostasis and reproduction; those of the lateral zone are involved with arousal and motivation.

The preoptic nuclei are involved with the release of gonadotropic hormones from the anterior pituitary gland (to be discussed later), and in temperature regulation.

The paraventricular and supraoptic nuclei will be considered together because they are both responsible for stimulating the secretion of the two major hormones of the posterior pituitary gland. The paraventricular nucleus stimulates the secretion of

○ Hypothalamic sulcus A	○ Fornix H	○ Infundibular nucleus M
○ Lamina terminalis B	○ Anterior pituitary I	○ Posterior nucleus N
○ Interpeduncular fossa C	○ Posterior pituitary I₁	○ Anterior nucleus O
○ Tuber cinereum D	○ Preoptic nucleus J	○ Dorsomedial nucleus P
○ Optic chiasm E	○ Suprachiasmatic nucleus K	○ Ventromedial nucleus Q
○ Mamillary bodies F	○ Paraventricular nucleus L	○ Supraoptic nucleus R
○ Infundibulum G		

oxytocin, a hormone that stimulates uterine contraction, from the posterior pituitary gland, while the supraoptic nucleus is responsible for the secretion of antidiuretic hormone (ADH, also known as arginine vasopressin), which acts on the kidneys to reabsorb water. For example, this is important when dehydration sets in and the body needs to hold on to more water.

The dorsomedial nucleus is involved with the stimulation of the gastrointestinal tract, and the ventromedial nucleus harbors a satiety center, which informs the body when its hunger for food has been satiated. The infundibular (or arcuate) nucleus is involved in the production of hypothalamic releasing factors which, as you will soon see, are important to the neuroendocrine system. The posterior nucleus is involved with stimulating the sympathetic system, which is a division of the autonomic nervous system, and will be discussed later.

The suprachiasmatic nucleus is involved in the regulation of circadian rhythms and, as a result, receives direct input from the retina. The anterior nucleus is involved with the parasympathetic system, which is another division of the autonomic nervous system.

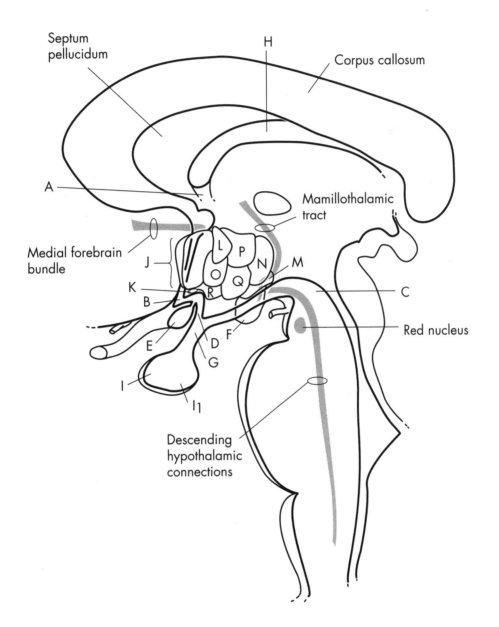

The nuclei of the hypothalamus

Chapter 7-4: Hypothalamus: Afferent Connections

The hypothalamus is integral to a variety of systems and, therefore, is closely connected to many different structures and systems. Hypothalamic afferent connections include the viscera (the organs of the body), the olfactory system, the cerebral cortex, the thalamus, the brainstem, and the retina. The major afferent connections, or pathways that bring neural signals, to the hypothalamus are discussed here.

The **median forebrain bundle (A)** passes through the hypothalamus and is the communication highway between the limbic system and the midbrain. It is composed of a bundle of nerve fibers that arises from the olfactory region, and the **septal nuclei (B)**; and as it passes through the hypothalamus it gives off septo-hypothalamic fibers from the septal area, olfacto-hypothalamic fibers from the olfactory region of the forebrain, and cortico-hypothalamic fibers from the orbiotofrontal cortex. The median forebrain bundle is the principal fiber system of the hypothalamus.

The **amygdalo-hypothalamic tract (C)** arises from the **amygdaloid nucleus (C$_1$)** and extends as the **stria terminalis (C$_2$)** over the thalamus, then projects to most of the hypothalamic nuclei anterior to the mamillary bodies and, finally, terminates in the preoptic area. Note that this is yet another hypothalamic link to the limbic system, as the amygdala is a limbic structure.

[Color C, C$_1$, and C$_2$ different shades of the same color.]

The **hippocampal-hypothalamic tract (D)** arises from the **hippocampus (D$_1$)** and forms the **crus of the fornix (D$_2$)**, which travels dorsally as the **body of the fornix (D$_3$)** and below the **corpus callosum (E)**, assuming a shape similar to it. The hippocampal-hypothalamic tract lies superior to the **thalamus (F)**, and at this point it curves inferiorly and ventrally as the **anterior column of the fornix (D$_4$)**, just after it gives off branches to the **anterior nucleus of the thalamus (G)**. Each of the anterior columns of the fornix enter the corresponding lateral wall of the third ventricle and most of the fibers end in the mamillary bodies.

[Color all of the D's the same color, and color F and G different shades of the same color.]

○ Median forebrain bundle A	○ Stria terminalis C$_2$	○ Anterior column of the fornix D$_4$
○ Septal nuclei B	○ Hippocampal-hypothalamic tract D	○ Corpus callosum E
○ Amygdalo-hypothalamic tract C	○ Hippocampus D$_1$	○ Thalamus F
○ Amygdaloid nucleus C$_1$	○ Crus of the fornix D$_2$	○ Anterior nucleus of the thalamus G
	○ Body of the fornix D$_3$	

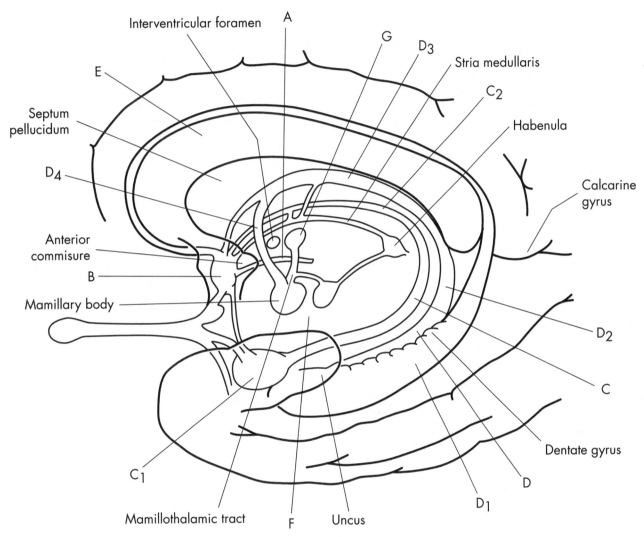

Interventricular foramen

A

G

D3

Stria medullaris

E

C2

Septum
pellucidum

Habenula

D4

Calcarine
gyrus

Anterior
commisure

B

Mamillary body

D2

C

C1

Dentate gyrus

D

Mamillothalamic tract

F

Uncus

D1

Hypothalamus: Afferent connections

Chapter 7-5: Hypothalamus: Efferent Connections

Many of the efferent connections of the hypothalamus are simply opposite to the afferent connections, which we just discussed; the efferent connections carry signals from the hypothalamus to other structures. The major efferent connections include the median forebrain bundle (shown previously), the **mammillothalamic tract (A)**, the **mammillotegmental tract (B)**, the **tuberoinfundibular tract (C)**, and the hypothalamic-hypophyseal tract (discussed along with the hypothalamo-hypophyseal portal system).

[Trace over A, B, and C in different colors.]

The median forebrain bundle and the dorsal longitudinal fasciculus both carry signals from the lateral hypothalamus to the midbrain tegmentum; the median forebrain also carries signals from the hypothalamus to the septal nuclei.

The mammillothalamic tract and the mammillotegmental tract both arise from the mammillary fasciculus and, after passing through the hypothalamus, travel to the anterior nucleus of the thalamus and the midbrain tegmentum, respectively. In this way they both provide a pathway for hypothalamic efferent fibers.

The tubuloinfundibular tract travels from the infundibular nucleus (which was discussed previously) to the hypophyseal portal system (to be discussed later). This is logical, because the infundibular hypothalamic nucleus is involved in the production of hypothalamic releasing factors.

Clinical Correlates: *Lesions of the hypothalamus can cause a wide array of defects, including sleep disturbances and difficulties in temperature regulation. Since you are now familiar with the function of each of the major hypothalamic nuclei, you should be able to predict what type of difficulties would arise if a particular nucleus were damaged. For instance, if the supraoptic nuclei were damaged, you would expect a deficiency in the secretion of ADH, which results in a condition known as diabetes insipidus. This lack of ADH prevents the effective reabsorption of water from the kidneys into the intravascular system. As a result, very dilute urine is produced and dehydration results. Note that this is not to be confused with diabetes mellitus, which is a disorder of glucose metabolism. Lesions of the preoptic nuclei, a nuclei that is normally involved in temperature control, could produce hyperthermia, as the mechanisms for cooling down, which help maintain normal body temperature would be impaired. Other disorders involving the hypothalamus, namely neuroendocrine disorders, are the result of damage to the hypothalamic-hypophyseal portal system.*

○ Mammillothalamic tract   A   ○ Mammillotegmental tract   B   ○ Tuberoinfundibular tract   C

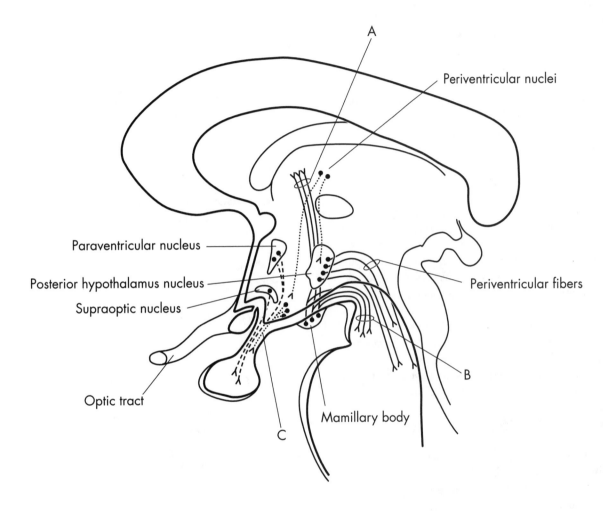

A

Periventricular nuclei

Paraventricular nucleus

Posterior hypothalamus nucleus

Supraoptic nucleus

Periventricular fibers

Optic tract

B

Mamillary body

C

Hypothalamus: Efferent connections

Chapter 7-6: Hypothalamic-Hypophyseal Portal System

The **pituitary gland (A)**, which works closely with the hypothalamus, is responsible for the secretion of a number of hormones that are vital to various organ systems. This small oval gland lies at the base of the brain, in a pocket of the sphenoid bone known as the sella turcica. The pituitary gland is also named the hypophysis and consists of two divisions, one anterior and one posterior. The **anterior pituitary (B)** is also known as the adenohypophysis, and the **posterior pituitary (C)** is known as the neurohypophysis. The two differ in size, physiological function, and embryologic origin.

[Color B and C different shades of the same color.]

The adenohypophysis constitutes approximately 80% of the pituitary gland and originates from Rathke's pouch, which is an invagination of pharyngeal epithelium; for this reason, the adenohypophysis contains glandular epithelial cells. The neurohypophysis is derived from an outpouching of the hypothalamus and is of neural origin; it contains axons that arise from neurons in the hypothalamus.

The pituitary gland secretes a number of hormones, all of which are regulated by hypothalamic regulatory hormones manufactured in the hypothalamus. These regulatory hormones are the hypothalamic releasing hormones and hypothalamic inhibiting hormones. With the exception of prolactin, which is regulated by an inhibitory hormone, and growth hormone (GH), which responds to both inhibitory and releasing hormones, the hormones of the anterior pituitary respond to the hypothalamic releasing hormones. They reach the anterior pituitary via the **hypophyseal portal veins (D)**. In the anterior pituitary, the group of cells that is responsible for the secretion of a certain hormone is stimulated by the appropriate hypothalamic regulatory hormone. Once stimulated, the group secretes the hormone, which then acts on a specific organ, known as its target organ. The target organ then secretes its particular hormone(s).

A feedback system exists that helps regulate the rate of hormonal secretion: If there is an excess of a particular hormone in the blood, that hormone will feed back to the hypothalamus and the pituitary and instruct them to decrease their rates of secretion.

This process is called negative feedback, and it occurs in all hormonal systems of the body. For example, the hypothalamus secretes thyrotropin-releasing hormone (TRH), which acts on the group of adenohypophyseal cells responsible for secreting the hormone that TRH regulates—thyroid-stimulating hormone (TSH). TSH is then secreted by the anterior pituitary and acts upon its target organ—the thyroid gland. The thyroid gland then secretes its hormone, thyroxine. But say that an excess of thyroxine in the bloodstream occurs. In this case, thyroxine feeds back to the hypothalamus and the anterior pituitary and instructs them to decrease their rate of secretion of TRH and TSH.

The following table lists the major hypothalamic and anterior pituitary releasing and inhibitory hormones.

As we stated earlier, the posterior pituitary is of neural origin and the anterior pituitary is not. The anterior pituitary is connected to the hypothalamus via the portal circulation, which is a network of arteries and capillaries that drain into the anterior pituitary from the hypothalamus; the portal veins bring hypothalamic releasing and inhibiting hormones from the hypothalamus to the anterior pituitary. Also, the anterior pituitary hormones are manufactured within the anterior pituitary, but the posterior pituitary hormones are manufactured in the hypothalamus, and then transported via the axons, not the blood vessels, of the **infundibulum (E)** (the pituitary stalk) to the posterior pituitary for storage and subsequent release. Release of these hormones is not regulated by hypothalamic hormones secreted into the portal circulation, but by nerve signals from the hypothalamus that travel to the posterior pituitary via a neuronal tract called the **hypothalamic-hypophyseal portal tract (F)**. The two principal hormones secreted by the posterior pituitary are oxytocin and vasopressin (also called antidiuretic hormone—ADH), which are synthesized by the **paraventricular (G)** and **supraoptic (H) hypothalamic nuclei**. Oxytocin stimulates contraction of the uterus during labor and stimulates contractile cells of the breast during milk ejection. Vasopressin acts on the kidney to reabsorb, and thus decrease the excretion of, water, and is therefore also known as antidiuretic hormone (ADH).

[Color G and H different colors.]

○	Pituitary gland	A	○	Hypophyseal portal veins	D
○	Anterior pituitary	B	○	Infundibulum	E
○	Posterior pituitary	C	○	Hypothalamic-hypophyseal portal tract	F
			○	Paraventricular hypothalamic nuclei	G
			○	Supraoptic hypothalamic nuclei	H

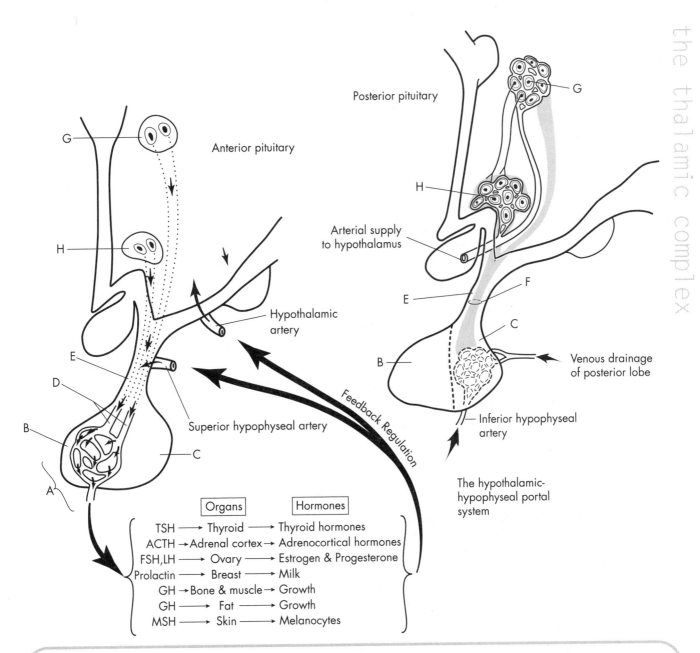

Anterior pituitary

Posterior pituitary

G

H

Arterial supply
to hypothalamus

Hypothalamic
artery

E

F

C

B

Venous drainage
of posterior lobe

Inferior hypophyseal
artery

E

D

B

Superior hypophyseal artery

Feedback Regulation

A

C

The hypothalamic-
hypophyseal portal
system

| Organs | Hormones |

TSH → Thyroid → Thyroid hormones
ACTH → Adrenal cortex → Adrenocortical hormones
FSH,LH → Ovary → Estrogen & Progesterone
Prolactin → Breast → Milk
GH → Bone & muscle → Growth
GH → Fat → Growth
MSH → Skin → Melanocytes

HYPOTHALAMIC AND ANTERIOR PITUITARY HORMONES

Hypothalamic Releasing and Inhibiting Hormones	Action of Hypothalamic Hormones on Anterior Pituitary	Target Organ and Function of Anterior Pituitary Hormones
Corticotropin-releasing hormone (CRH)	Stimulates release of adrenocorticotropic hormone (ACTH)	ACTH stimulates adrenal gland to secrete glucocorticoids and androgens
Gonadotropin-releasing hormone (GnRH)	Stimulates release of follicle-stimulating hormone (FSH) and leutinizing hormone (LH)	FSH and LH act on the ovaries and testes to stimulate ovarian follicle development, spermatogenesis, and steroidogenesis
Thyrotropin-releasing hormone (TRH)	Stimulates release of thyroid-stimulating hormone (TSH).	TSH stimulates the thyroid gland to secrete thyroxine
Growth hormone-releasing hormone (GHRH)	Stimulates release of growth hormone (GH)	GH has no specific target gland but acts on almost all tissues of the body, promoting growth and influencing metabolism.
Growth hormone-inhibiting hormone (GHIH) (Somatostatin)	Inhibits release of growth hormone (GH)	As above
Prolactin inhibitory factor (PIF)	Inhibits release of prolactin. This factor is believed to be dopamine	Prolactin is involved with the initiation of milk production by the mammary glands.

Chapter 7-7: Epithalamus and Subthalamus

The epithalamus sits at the posterior aspect of the thalamus, underneath the **splenium of the corpus callosum (A)**. The structures of the epithalamus include the **habenula (B)** and the **pineal body (C)**. The habenula is a bundle of nerve cells that lies near the ventral surface of the thalamus. It receives input from the septal nuclei, the lateral preoptic nuclei, the anterior thalamic nuclei, and the globus pallidus, via a nerve bundle known as the **stria medullaris (D)**. The pineal gland (which resembles a pine cone) lies just beneath the roof of the third ventricle and superior to the superior colliculi. Note that it is a single structure that lies in the midline; it is involved in the control of circadian rhythms and works in conjunction with the suprachiasmatic nucleus of the hypothalamus. The pineal gland is virtually devoid of nerve cells and, therefore, does not contain central neural connections. It contains and secretes a high concentration of melatonin and a neurotransmitter called serotonin.

[Color A-D different colors.]

The **subthalamic nucleus (E)** lies inferoposterior to the **thalamus (F)**, and medial to the internal capsule, which separates it from the globus pallidus. The subthalamus cannot be clearly viewed on gross section because it lies deep within the diencephalon. It is located ventral to the thalamus, lateral to the hypothalamus, and medial to the internal capsule. The subthalamus, like the substantia nigra, is considered a physiologic component of the basal ganglia because it works with the basal ganglia to modulate motor control.

[Color E and F different shades of the same color.]

Clinical Correlates: *As we discussed previously, damage to the subthalamic nucleus has been known to produce a condition known as hemiballismus, a condition in which the individual suffers violent and uncontrollable flailing movements of the contralateral (opposite) limb or limbs.*

○ Splenium of the corpus callosum	A	○ Pineal body	C	○ Subthalamic nucleus	E
○ Habenula	B	○ Stria medullaris	D	○ Thalamus	F

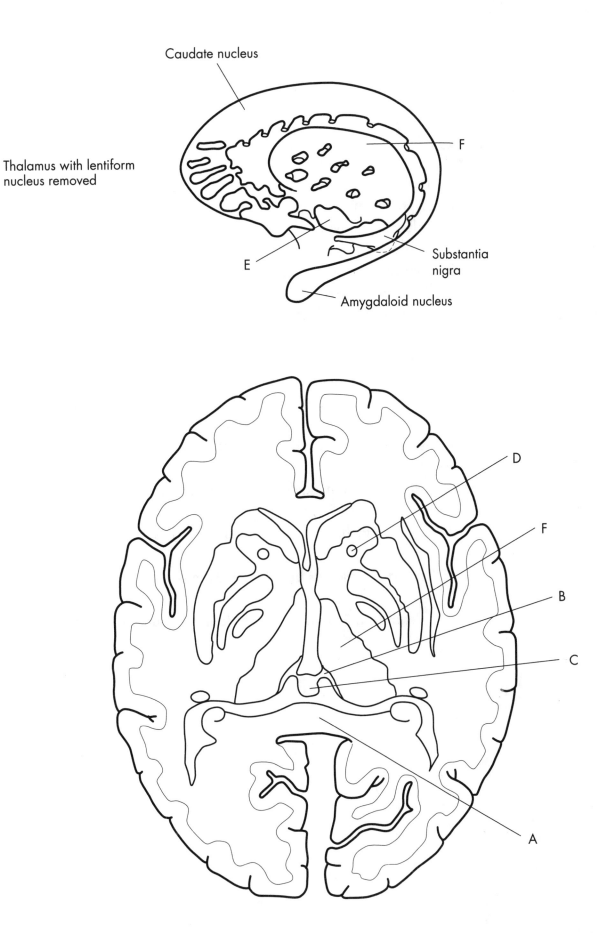

Caudate nucleus

Thalamus with lentiform
nucleus removed

F

E

Substantia
nigra

Amygdaloid nucleus

D

F

B

C

A

THE THALAMIC COMPLEX
self assessment

A. Thalamus
B. Hypothalamus
C. Adenohypophysis
D. Neurohypophysis
E. Suprachiasmatic nucleus
F. Posterior nucleus
G. Ventromedial nucleus
H. Stria terminalis
I. Lamina terminalis
J. Hypothalamic sulcus
K. Subthalamic nucleus

1. Secretes antidiuretic hormone (ADH)

2. Extension of amygdalo-hypothalamic tract

3. Damage to this structure causes hemiballismus

4. Separates thalamus from hypothalamus

5. Extends from lamina terminalis to interpeduncular fossa

CHAPTER EIGHT

the
basal
ganglia

Chapter 8-1: Lateral Views

The basal ganglia are masses of gray matter that lie lateral to the thalamus; they are present in each of the cerebral hemispheres and are primarily composed of the following structures: the **caudate nucleus (A)**, the **putamen (B)**, and the **globus pallidus (C)**. The putamen and globus pallidus are collectively referred to as the **lentiform nucleus** (or lenticular nucleus) **(D)**, and the caudate and putamen are collectively referred to as the **corpus striatum (E)**; they are essentially a continuous structure.

[Color A, B, and C different colors.]

The caudate nucleus is a C-shaped structure. The two ends of the C point anteriorly and the spine of the C points posteriorly when it is viewed from the side. The top, free end of the C is referred to as the **head of caudate (A$_1$)**, the bottom, free end is the **tail of caudate (A$_2$)**, and the entire curved portion in-between is the **body of caudate (A$_3$)**. The head of the caudate lies anterior to the **thalamus (F)** and forms the floor of the **anterior horn of the lateral ventricle (G)**; the body of the caudate forms part of the floor of the **body of the lateral ventricle (H)**; the tail of the caudate occupies the roof of the **inferior horn of the lateral ventricle (I)**, and ends in the **amygdaloid nucleus (J)**. The lateral side of the caudate nucleus is separated from the lentiform nucleus by the **internal capsule (K)**, which is a dense band of afferent (going toward the CNS) and efferent (going away from the CNS) nerve fibers that connects the brainstem and spinal cord to the cerebral cortex. However, this separation is incomplete because the head of the caudate is connected to the putamen anteroinferiorly.

[Color A$_1$, A$_2$, and A$_3$ different shades of the same color.
Color G, H, and I different shades of a darker color.]

The lentiform nucleus (remember, the putamen and globus pallidus) is a wedge-shaped structure that sits lateral to the internal capsule. It is oriented in such a way that its wide base points laterally (toward the outside of the brain) and its apex points medially (toward the inside of the brain). The globus pallidus can be distinguished from the putamen by (1) its more medial location, and (2) its pale color, which is due to the fact that it contains a greater number of myelinated nerve fibers.

The basal ganglia are primarily involved in the regulation of motor control, and they work closely with the corticospinal tract to perform this function—this may be why the internal capsule is so close to the basal ganglia. Afferent connections to the corpus striatum arise from the cerebral cortex, brainstem, and substantia nigra; acetylcholine, serotonin, and dopamine are the primary neurotransmitters used for the transmission of neural impulses from these areas, respectively. Efferent fibers from the corpus striatum travel to the globus pallidus and substantia nigra; the primary neurotransmitter used by this pathway is GABA (gamma-aminobutyric acid). The basal ganglia act as companions to the cerebral cortex in the execution of previously learned movements and the planning of complex, new movements. They are involved in the regulation of motor activity rather than its initiation; motor activity is usually initiated in the motor areas of the cortex. For instance, the basal ganglia are involved in actions such as typing and, in addition, they modulate the form in which these patterns of movements are executed (i.e. typing fast versus slow). There are different neural loops within the basal ganglia themselves as well as between them and other parts of the brain, and if any one of the structures in the circuit becomes defective, the entire system can be damaged.

Clinical Correlates: *A well-known movement disorder is Parkinson's disease. Parkinson's results from the deterioration of the substantia nigra. Since neurons of the nigrostriatal pathway (that travels from the substantia nigra to the corpus striatum) secrete dopamine, and since dopamine is primarily an inhibitory neurotransmitter, it is believed that a deficiency of dopaminergic inhibition—which results from the degeneration of the substantia nigra—is the major cause of the symptoms of Parkinson's. The symptoms include slowed movement, rigidity, and tremor.*

Huntington's chorea is a movement disorder that results from the loss of GABA-secreting neurons in the caudate and putamen. GABA is an inhibitory neurotransmitter and since striatal axons that project to the globus pallidus and substantia nigra would secrete less GABA, a loss of inhibition results. This loss of inhibition produces a relative hyperexcited state that results in hyperkinesis (heightened muscular activity) and jerky movements of different parts of the body.

○ Caudate nucleus   A   ○ Globus pallidus   C   ○ Body of the lateral
                                                                        ventricle   H
○ Head of caudate   A₁   ○ Lentiform nucleus   D
                                                                     ○ Inferior horn of the
○ Tail of caudate   A₂   ○ Corpus striatum   E   lateral ventricle   I
○ Body of caudate   A₃   ○ Thalamus   F   ○ Amygdaloid nucleus   J
○ Putamen   B   ○ Anterior horn of the   ○ Internal capsule   K
                                      lateral ventricle   G

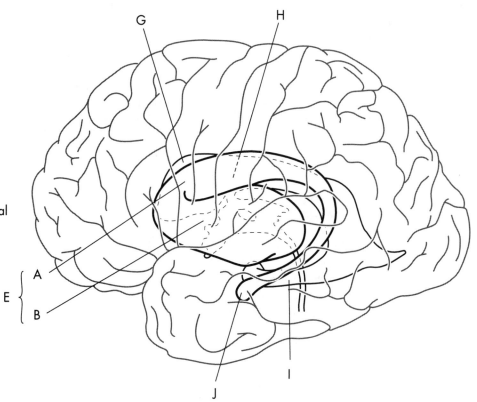

Location and
anatomy of basal
ganglia

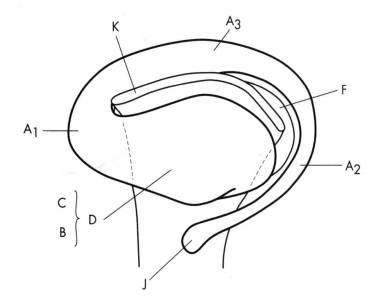

Parts of the
basal ganglia

Chapter 8-2: Three-Dimensional Views

These pictures should provide you with a somewhat 3-dimensional view of the anatomic relationships between the basal ganglia and the thalamus. In the top figure you will notice the intact basal ganglia with the bulging **putamen (A)** and rounded **caudate nucleus (B)**. Notice once again how the head of the caudate is connected to the putamen, and remember that only this part is not separated by the internal capsule. Once again, you see the **thalamus (C)**, on the same side as the caudate nucleus.

[Color A, B, and C a different color.]

The tail of the caudate fuses with the **amygdaloid body (D)**, which is an almond-shaped complex of nuclei that lies deep in the uncus (the anterior endpoint of the parahippocampal gyrus of the temporal lobe). The amygdala is involved with the expression of emotion and is a component of the limbic system; it has a great number of connections with the hypothalamus as well as with the limbic cortex and various other areas. Stimulation of the amygdala produces autonomic functions that are further controlled by the hypothalamus, such as pupillary dilation or contraction and modulation of the heart rate. Functions of movement also result from stimulation of the amygdala.

The **substantia nigra (E)** is a large, gray matter nucleus that extends throughout the entire midbrain. It is considered a *physiological*, rather than an anatomical, component of the basal ganglia. In other words, although it is not considered one of the basal ganglia structures, anatomically speaking, it works so closely with the basal ganglia in motor control that it is considered to be a functional relative (keep in mind, however, that the exact anatomic definition of the basal ganglia is loose and that some, therefore, do regard the substantia nigra as an anatomical member of the basal ganglia). One region of the substantia nigra called the pars compacta contains neurons that contain the dark pigment melanin, and it is for this reason that the substantia nigra is dark in color. The cells of the pars compacta also contain a rich concentration of the neurotransmitter dopamine; you may recall that dopamine is a prominent neurotransmitter in the basal ganglia circuit.

[You should color E black.]

The middle figure shows the thalamus after the lentiform nucleus and amygdaloid body have been removed. This view will allow you to appreciate the anatomic relationship between the thalamus and the basal ganglia. Another important structure that is unveiled by this view is the **subthalamic nucleus (F)**, which is a nucleus of the subthalamus that lies inferoposterior to the thalamus. The subthalamus, like the substantia nigra, is considered a physiologic component of the basal ganglia because it works with the basal ganglia to modulate motor control.

In the bottom figure, you will notice a thin sheet of gray matter lateral to the putamen; it is called the **claustrum (G)**. The claustrum is separated from the putamen by the insular cortex, to which the putamen sits just medial. Also separating the claustrum from the putamen is a thin layer of white matter known as the external capsule—the external capsule is not shown. This external capsule also separates the claustrum from the insular cortex. Therefore, moving in a medial to lateral direction you have the putamen, the external capsule, the claustrum, the extreme capsule, and the insular cortex. Note also that the external and extreme capsules are composed of white matter and that the claustrum is composed of gray matter. The exact function of the claustrum has not yet been determined.

Clinical Correlates: Klüver-Bucy Syndrome *is often seen in monkeys but is rare in man; it results from a destruction of the anterior segments of both temporal lobes; this also destroys the amygdalas, which inhibit this region. A certain set of behaviors arise as a result of this disorder, such as complete fearlessness, extreme hypersexuality, decreased aggressiveness, and the need to examine things orally. Damage to the subthalamic nucleus has been known to produce a condition known as hemiballismus, in which the individual suffers violent and uncontrollable flailing movements of the contralateral (opposite) limb(s). In other words, if the lesion occurred in the subthalamic nucleus of the left cerebral hemisphere, the flailing movements would take place in the right limb(s).*

○ Putamen	A	○ Amygdaloid body	D	○ Subthalamic nucleus	F
○ Caudate nucleus	B	○ Substantia nigra	E	○ Claustrum	G
○ Thalamus	C				

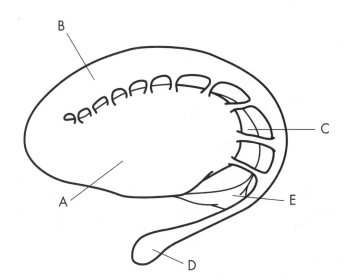

Lateral view of
basal ganglia

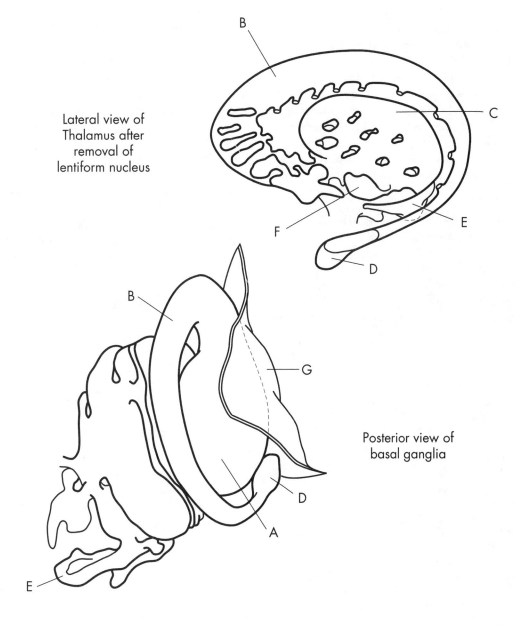

Lateral view of
Thalamus after
removal of
lentiform nucleus

Posterior view of
basal ganglia

Chapter 8-3: Projection Fibers and Horizontal Section

The cortical white matter of the brain is composed of a fan-shaped bundle of nerve fibers that convey impulses between the cerebral cortex and the brainstem; these fibers are called projection fibers, and they are collectively known as the **corona radiata (A)**. Near the top of the brainstem these fibers taper to form the internal capsule, which carries all of the nerve fibers to and from the cerebral cortex. The internal capsule is composed of three segments: the **anterior limb of internal capsule (B)**, a longer **posterior limb of internal capsule (B$_1$)**, and the **genu of internal capsule (B$_2$)**. The anterior limb separates the head of the caudate from the lentiform nucleus, while the posterior limb separates the lentiform nucleus from the thalamus. This can be seen more clearly in the horizontal section. The head of the caudate lies medial to the anterior limb, the thalamus lies medial to the posterior limb, and the lentiform nucleus lies lateral to both limbs. The genu of the internal capsule is formed by the impingement of the pointed apex of the wedge-shaped lentiform nucleus onto the internal capsule, which causes it to bend.

[Use a different color for A and B. Use different shades of the same color for B, B$_1$, and B$_2$.]

Note in the horizontal section, the **head (C)** and **tail (C$_1$)** of the caudate nucleus. The head of the caudate makes up the floor of the **anterior horn of the lateral ventricle (D)** and for this reason the caudate it is situated immediately adjacent to the anterior horn of the lateral ventricle. In addition, note that the caudate lies anterior to the **thalamus (E)**. The relationship between the body of the caudate and the lateral ventricle will be discussed later. Notice the tail of the caudate, which occupies the roof of the inferior horn of the lateral ventricle (not shown).

[Use different shades of the same color for C and C$_1$.]

The **putamen (F)** and the **globus pallidus (G)** can also be seen clearly in the horizontal section. Notice once again that the internal capsule separates the caudate from the lentiform nucleus in all places but at the head of the caudate, which is continuous with the putamen. In cross section, note the **claustrum (H)**, and the **external capsule (I)**, which separates the claustrum from the putamen. Also note the **insular cortex (J)**, which is located just lateral to the claustrum.

Other structures labeled in the cross-sectional diagram include: the **genu of corpus callosum (K)**, the **cerebellar hemispheres (L)**, the **cerebellar vermis (M)**, the **inferior colliculus (N)**, the **superior colliculus (O)**, the **pineal body (P)**, the **third ventricle (Q)**, the **anterior column of fornix (R)**, and the **septum pellucidum (S)**. These structures are included only to help you orient yourself; they will be discussed later.

[Use different colors for K-S, with the exception of N and O. For these two use different shades of the same color.]

○	Corona radiata	A	○	Anterior horn of the lateral ventricle	D	○	Cerebellar hemispheres	L
○	Anterior limb of internal capsule	B	○	Thalamus	E	○	Cerebellar vermis	M
○	Posterior limb of internal capsule	B$_1$	○	Putamen	F	○	Inferior colliculus	N
○	Genu of internal capsule	B$_2$	○	Globus pallidus	G	○	Superior colliculus	O
○	Head of caudate nucleus	C	○	Claustrum	H	○	Pineal body	P
○	Tail of caudate nucleus	C$_1$	○	External capsule	I	○	Third ventricle	Q
			○	Insular cortex	J	○	Anterior column of fornix	R
			○	Genu of corpus callosum	K	○	Septum pellucidum	S

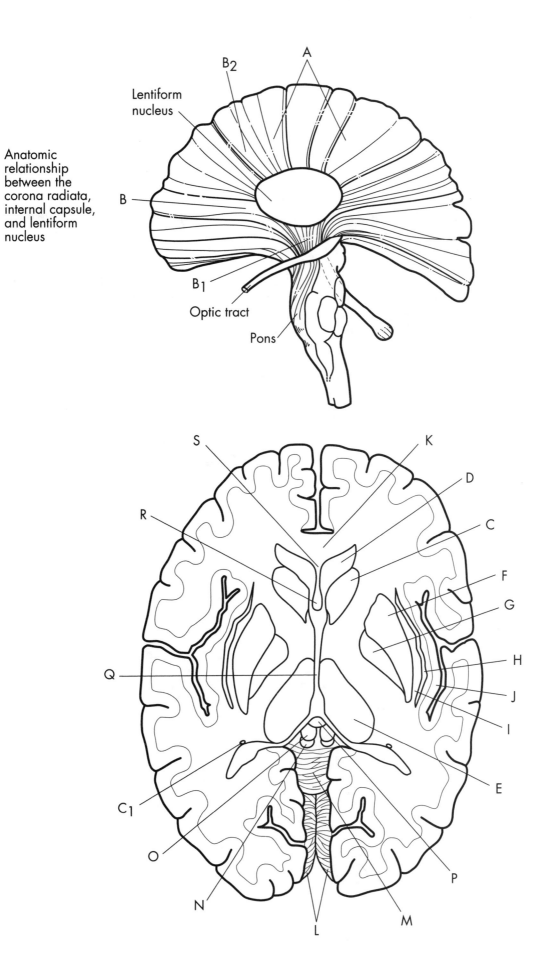

A

B₂

Lentiform
nucleus

B

B₁

Optic tract

Pons

Anatomic
relationship
between the
corona radiata,
internal capsule,
and lentiform
nucleus

S

R

Q

C₁

O

N

L

K

D

C

F

G

H

J

I

E

P

M

Horizontal
section of the
brain

Chapter 8-4: In Coronal Section

On the opposing page are the basal ganglia in coronal section. Having looked at the complete pictures of the basal ganglia on the previous pages should help you to understand these coronal sections. Recall that the head of the caudate nucleus forms the floor of the anterior horn of the lateral ventricles. Since the top figure is a section through the anterior horn of the lateral ventricle, you can see the **head of the caudate nucleus (A)**. You can also see the **lentiform nucleus (B)**, which is separated from the caudate by the **anterior limb of the internal capsule (C)**. Immediately adjacent to the head of the caudate lies the **anterior horn of the lateral ventricle (D)**. Because this coronal section is taken from an anterior portion of the brain, you can see the **genu of the corpus callosum (E)**; this is its anterior-most portion, where it bends inferiorly.

[Color A-E different colors.]

Note the **body of the lateral ventricle (D_1)** in the bottom figure, and recall that the **body of the caudate nucleus (A_1)** forms part of the floor of the body of the lateral ventricle. Notice also the **body of the corpus callosum (E_1)**, which forms the roof of the lateral ventricles. You may recall that the **tail of the caudate nucleus (A_2)** forms the roof of the **inferior horn of the lateral ventricle (D_2)**.

[Color all of the A's different shades of the same colors. Do the same for all of the C's, D's and E's.]

Now look at the **thalamus (F)**, and notice that it is separated from the lentiform nucleus by the **posterior limb of the internal capsule (C_1)**. Once again, notice the **claustrum (G)**, which lies between the putamen and the **insular cortex (H)**. Also note the **subthalamic nucleus (I)** and the **substantia nigra (J)**.

○ Head of the caudate nucleus   A

○ Body of the caudate nucleus A_1

○ Tail of the caudate nucleus A_2

○ Lentiform nucleus   B

○ Anterior limb of the internal capsule   C

○ Posterior limb of the internal capsule C_1

○ Anterior horn of the lateral ventricle   D

○ Body of the lateral ventricle D_1

○ Inferior horn of the lateral ventricle D_2

○ Genu of the corpus callosum   E

○ Body of the corpus callosum E_1

○ Thalamus   F

○ Claustrum   G

○ Insular cortex   H

○ Subthalamic nucleus   I

○ Substantia nigra   J

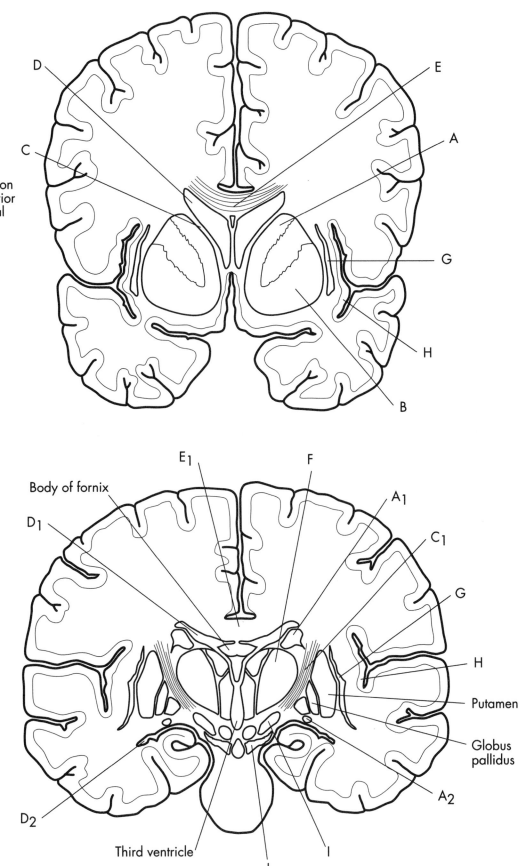

D

C

E

A

Coronal section
through anterior
horn of lateral
ventricle

G

H

B

E₁

Body of fornix

F

A₁

D₁

C₁

G

H

Coronal
section
through
ventral
portion of
pons

Putamen

Globus
pallidus

A₂

D₂

Third ventricle

J

I

Chapter 8-5: Neuronal Connections

In this section we will discuss the afferent and efferent connections that involve the **caudate nucleus (A)**, the **putamen (B)**, the **globus pallidus (C)**, the **substantia nigra (D)**, the **thalamus (E)**, and the **cerebral cortex (F)**. Each of these connections ends on top of the structure that the connection is projecting to, and inside this block is the neurotransmitter that is used in the particular connection. Let us first discuss the afferent and efferent connections of the striatum, and move on to those of the globus pallidus.

[Use one color for the connections of each structure.]

Afferent fibers of the striatum (the caudate and putamen) come primarily from the cerebral cortex, the substantia nigra, and the thalamus. For this reason, they are known, respectively, as corticostriate fibers, nigrostriate fibers, and thalamostriate fibers. Corticostriate fibers arise from almost all parts of the cerebral cortex, and each portion of the cerebral cortex projects to a specific site of the striatum; most fibers arise from the ipsilateral (same side) cerebral cortex, meaning that most of the corticostriate fibers that converge on the right striatum came from the right cerebral cortex. Most such fibers arise from an area of the cerebral cortex known as the sensorimotor cortex. The primary neurotransmitter used in this pathway is glutamate.

The nigrostriate fibers travel from the **pars compacta (G)** of the substantia nigra to the caudate nucleus and putamen. Dopamine is the primary neurotransmitter used in this pathway. Thalamostriate fibers run from the thalamus to the caudate and putamen, and the primary neurotransmitter is glutamate.

The efferent fibers of the striatum include the striatopallidal fibers and the striatonigral fibers. The striatopallidal fibers travel from the caudate nucleus and putamen to the globus pallidus. The primary neurotransmitter used here is gamma-aminobutyric acid (GABA), which is an inhibitory neurotransmitter. The striatonigral fibers travel from the caudate and putamen to the **pars reticularis (H)** and the substantia nigra. The neurotransmitters here vary between the different groups of fibers; they include GABA, acetylcholine, and substance P.

The afferent connections of the globus pallidus include the subthalamopallidal fibers and the aforementioned striatopallidal fibers. The subthalamopallidal fibers project to the globus pallidus from the subthalamic nucleus and use glutamate as their primary neurotransmitter.

The major efferent fibers of the globus pallidus include the **ansa lenticularis (I)**, the **fasciculus lenticularis (J)**, and the pallidotegmental fibers (not shown). The ansa lenticularis fibers travel from the globus pallidus to the thalamus, using GABA as their primary neurotransmitter. The fasciculus lenticularis fibers travel from the globus pallidus to the subthalamus, and also use GABA as their primary neurotransmitter.

○ Caudate nucleus	A	○ Substantia nigra	D	○ Pars reticularis	H
○ Putamen	B	○ Thalamus	E	○ Ansa lenticularis	I
○ Globus pallidus	C	○ Cerebral cortex	F	○ Fasciculus lenticularis	J
		○ Pars compacta	G		

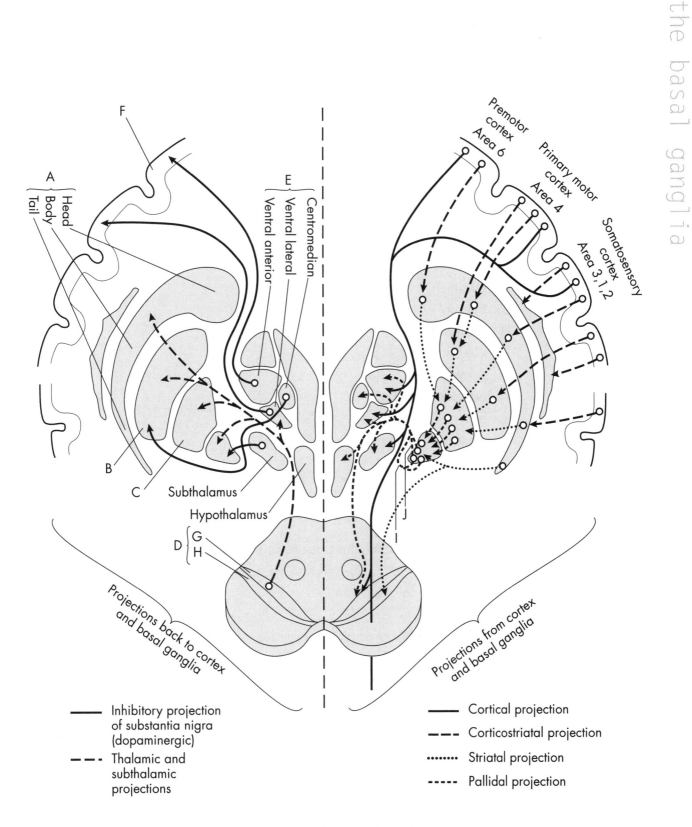

F

A { Head
    Body
    Tail

E { Centromedian
    Ventral lateral
    Ventral anterior

Premotor
cortex
Area 6

Primary motor
cortex
Area 4

Somatosensory
cortex
Area 3, 1, 2

B

C

Subthalamus

Hypothalamus

D { G
    H

J

I

Projections back to cortex
and basal ganglia

Projections from cortex
and basal ganglia

——— Inhibitory projection
of substantia nigra
(dopaminergic)

– – – Thalamic and
subthalamic
projections

——— Cortical projection

– – – Corticostriatal projection

········· Striatal projection

- - - - Pallidal projection

The connections of the basal ganglia

THE BASAL GANGLIA

self assessment

A. Head of caudate nucleus
B. Body of caudate nucleus
C. Tail of caudate nucleus
D. Globus pallidus
E. Anterior horn of lateral ventricle
F. Putamen
G. Internal capsule
H. Claustrum
I. Neurohypophysis
J. Amygdaloid nucleus
K. Substantia nigra
L. Insular cortex
M. Ansa lenticularis

1. Occupies roof of inferior horn of lateral ventricle

2. Damage to this structure results in Parkinson's disease

3. Lies lateral to claustrum

4. Efferent pathway of globus pallidus

5. Separates putamen from insular cortex

CHAPTER NINE

the
brain
stem

Chapter 9-1: The Midbrain

The brain stem encompasses the midbrain, the **pons (A)**, and the **medulla oblongata (B)** and connects the cerebellum and pons to the forebrain. The midbrain, which is the smallest part of the brain stem, lies between the cerebrum and the pons; its roof is formed by the **superior colliculi (C)** and the **inferior colliculi (D)**. The superior colliculi deal with the visual reflex and have fibers that travel to the **lateral geniculate body (E)**, and the inferior colliculi deal with auditory reflex and have fibers that travel to the **medial geniculate body (E_1)**.

[Color C and D different shades of the same color. Do the same for E and E_1.]

As you can see in the bottom diagram, the **cerebral aqueduct (G)** passes through the midbrain. The lower and larger portion of the midbrain contains the **cerebral peduncles (F)**, which are divided into the anterior **tegmentum (H)**, and a posterior **crus cerebri (I)**; the structure that divides the two sections is the pigmented, dopamine-rich **substantia nigra (J)**, which works closely with the basal ganglia to perform motor functions. The tegmentum contains a number of structures, which include the following: the **red nucleus (K)**, the trochlear nucleus (not shown), the **medial longitudinal fasciculus (L)**, the **oculomotor nucleus (M)**, the subthalamic nucleus (not shown), and the **reticular formation (N)**. The reticular formation spans all three segments of the brain stem and is involved in causing arousal from sleep. The **oculomotor nerve (M_1)** arises from the **interpeduncular fossa (O)**, which is located between the crus cerebri. The crus cerebri primarily consists of fibers from descending neuronal tracts that project to the spinal cord, pons, and lower brain stem. Cerebellar output fibers pass through the midbrain, forming the **superior cerebellar peduncles (P)**.

[Color J black and K red. Color M and M_1 different shades of the same color.]

Clinical Correlates: *One of the ways in which damage may occur to the midbrain is via an infarction. An infarction is simply the death of tissue as a result of a blockage of the blood supply (i.e. a clot in an artery) that supplies that piece of tissue. An infarction that damages the third cranial nerve in the midbrain may produce signs such as diplopia (double vision) and ptosis (eye-lid droop).*

○	Pons	A	○	Cerebral peduncles	F	○ Medial longitudinal fasciculus	L
○	Medulla oblongata	B	○	Cerebral aqueduct	G	○ Oculomotor nucleus	M
○	Superior colliculi	C	○	Tegmentum	H	○ Oculomotor nerve	M_1
○	Inferior colliculi	D	○	Crus cerebri	I	○ Reticular formation	N
○	Lateral geniculate body	E	○	Substantia nigra	J	○ Interpeduncular fossa	O
○	Medial geniculate body	E_1	○	Red nucleus	K	○ Superior cerebellar peduncles	P

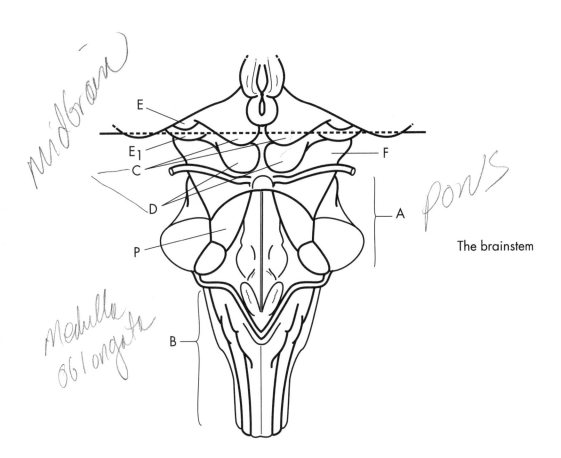

midbrain

Pons

Medulla Oblongata

The brainstem

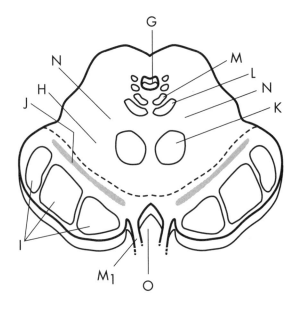

Section through the midbrain at level of superior colliculi

Chapter 9-2: The Pons

The pons lies anterior to the medulla and cerebellum and connects the medulla to the midbrain; its dorsal surface is formed by the floor of the **fourth ventricle (A)**. You can think of it as a bridge that connects the brain to the spinal cord and one cerebral hemisphere to the other. Transverse nerve fibers that travel from the pontine nuclei to the cerebellum form the largest of the cerebellar peduncles, the **middle cerebellar peduncles (B)**. Transverse sections of the pons show a larger anterior pontine portion, the tegmentum, and a smaller posterior portion. Within the tegmentum lie several structures, among which are: the **trigeminal nuclei (C)**, the **reticular formation (D)**, which lies in all three segments of the brain stem, and the **medial longitudinal fasciculus (E)**. In addition to the trigeminal nuclei, the pons also harbor the following cranial nerves and their nuclei: the **trigeminal nerve (F)**, the **facial nerve (G)**, the facial nucleus, the **vestibulocochlear nerve (H)**, the **abducens nerve (I)**, the abducens nucleus, and the vestibular and cochlear nuclei. The **medial lemniscus (J)** is located in the anterior part of the tegmentum, and the **lateral lemniscus (K)** lies just lateral to it; they form part of the dividing line between the anterior pontine tegmentum and the posterior pontine portion.

[Color J and K different shades of the same color. Color the remaining structures different colors.]

Clinical Correlates: *An infarct of the pons could damage the corticospinal fibers, and this would produce weakness in the contralateral side. If the abducens nerve were involved, the result would be weakness or paralysis of the lateral rectus muscle of the eye. Since the lateral rectus moves the eye laterally, the eye would deviate medially. An infarct could also involve the facial nerve, which would produce facial weakness on the side of the lesion.*

○ Fourth ventricle	A	○ Reticular formation	D	○ Vestibulocochlear nerve	H
○ Middle cerebellar peduncles	B	○ Medial longitudinal fasciculus	E	○ Abducens nerve	I
○ Trigeminal nuclei	C	○ Trigeminal nerve	F	○ Medial lemniscus	J
		○ Facial nerve	G	○ Lateral lemniscus	K

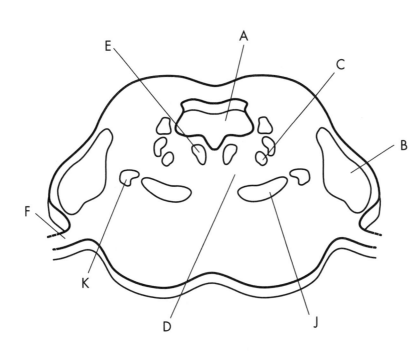

Section through
pons at level of
trigeminal nerves

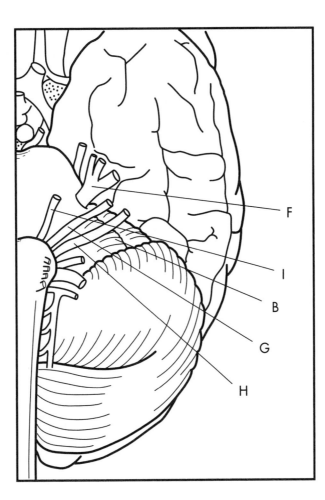

Anterior view of
brainstem

Chapter 9-3: The Medulla Oblongata

The **medulla oblongata (A)** is the rostral extention of the spinal cord; it connects the **pons (B)** to the spinal cord. It extends from the foramen magnum to the inferior border of the pons and contains all of the fibers of neuronal tracts that travel between the brain and spinal cord. The spinal canal continues into the caudal half of the medulla; the rostral half of the medulla contains the lower part of the **fourth ventricle (C)**, which is covered by the **inferior medullary vellum (D)**. Another continuation of the spinal cord that extends into the medulla is the **anterior median fissure (E)**, which is located on the ventral side of the medulla. On either side of the anterior median fissure are the medullary protuberances known as the **pyramids (F)**, which contain descending fibers of the corticospinal tract. Just above the point where the medulla and spinal cord meet is the area of corticospinal fiber known as the **pyramidal decussation (G)**. The following cranial nerves are present in the medulla: **glossopharyngeal (H)**, **vagus (I)**, **spinal accessory (J)**, and **hypoglossal (K)**.

[Color F and G different shades of the same color. Color the remaining structures different colors.]

On the dorsal side, the **posterior median sulcus (L)** can be seen at the midline of the medulla. The nuclei of the dorsal column pathway; the **nucleus gracilus (M)** and the **nucleus cuneatus (N)**, also lie on the dorsal aspect of the medulla. On either of the lateral walls of the medulla lie protuberances called the **olives (O)**, which are made up of the **inferior olivary nuclei (P)**. The inferior olivary nuclei send

fibers to the cerebellum and receive fibers from the cerebellum, basal ganglia, red nucleus, and cerebrum.

[Color M and N different shades of the same color.]

The diagram of the section through the rostral medulla at the level of the inferior olivary nuclei reveals a number of nuclei and tracts, including the following: the **vestibular nuclei (Q)**, the **nucleus of the solitary tract (R)**, the **hypoglossal nucleus (S)**, the inferior olivary nucleus, the **dorsal nucleus of the vagus (T)**, the **nucleus ambiguus (U)** of the reticular formation, the **cuneate nucleus (V)**, the **anterior spinocerebellar tract (W)**, the **posterior spinocerebellar tract (X)**, the **medial lemniscus (Y)**, and the **medial longitudinal fasciculus (Z)**.

[Color Q-Z different colors.]

Also within the medulla are areas vital to life, such as the cardiac and respiratory centers. The cardiac center helps to regulate the rhythmic contraction of the heart, and the respiratory center is involved with the modulation of breathing rhythms.

Clinical Correlates: *Damage to the medulla, through an infarction, for instance, can result in hemiparesis (paralysis of one side of the body) of the contralateral side as a result of damage to the corticospinal fibers. Head trauma to the base of the skull could damage the vital cardiac and respiratory centers of the medulla, causing death.*

○ Medulla oblongata	A	○ Spinal accessory nerve	J	○ Hypoglossal nucleus	S
○ Pons	B	○ Hypoglossal nerve	K	○ Dorsal nucleus of the vagus	T
○ Fourth ventricle	C	○ Posterior median sulcus	L	○ Nucleus ambiguus	U
○ Inferior medullary vellum	D	○ Nucleus gracilus	M	○ Cuneate nucleus	V
○ Anterior median fissure	E	○ Nucleus cuneatus	N	○ Anterior spino-cerebellar tract	W
○ Pyramids	F	○ Olives	O	○ Posterior spino-cerebellar tract	X
○ Pyramidal decussation	G	○ Inferior olivary nuclei	P	○ Medial lemniscus	Y
○ Glossopharyngeal nerve	H	○ Vestibular nuclei	Q	○ Medial longitudinal fasciculus	Z
○ Vagus nerve	I	○ Nucleus of the solitary tract	R		

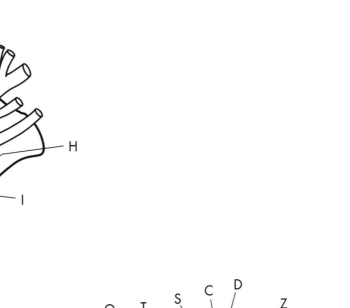

Anterior view of medulla
oblongata

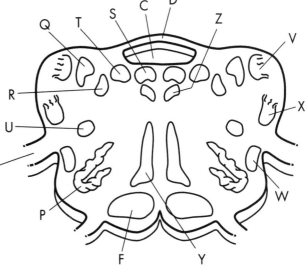

Section through medulla
oblongata at the inferior
olivary nuclei

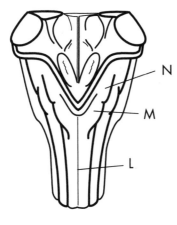

Posterior (dorsal) view of
medulla oblongata

CHAPTER
[9]

THE BRAIN STEM

self assessment

A. Pons
B. Nucleus gracilus
C. Pyramids
D. Thalamus
E. Spinal cord
F. Telencephalon
G. Medulla oblongata
H. Reticular formation
I. Midbrain
J. Optic nerve
K. Oculomotor nerve
L. Olfactory nerve

1. Middle cerebellar peduncles belong to this segment of the brain stem

2. Harbors trigeminal nuclei

3. Nerve arising from interpeduncular fossa

4. Superior cerebellar peduncles belong to this segment of brain stem

5. Harbors nuclei of dorsal column pathway

CHAPTER TEN

the cerebellum

Chapter 10-1: The Cerebellum

The cerebellum lies posterior to the pons and medulla and is the second-largest part of the brain. It is responsible for coordination of the unconscious, muscle movement, and maintaining balance and equilibrium. It receives input from essentially all parts of the brain and each of its hemispheres controls muscles on the same side of the body. Damage to the cerebellum does not cause muscle paralysis, but movements that are normally coordinated and smooth become erratic and unorganized.

The cerebellum occupies most of the posterior fossa of the cranium, and forms the roof of the **fourth ventricle (A)**. It is separated from the cerebrum by an extension of dura mater known in this area as the tentorium cerebelli, and consists of two hemispheres that are joined by a structure known as the **vermis (B)** whose anterior portion is called the **lingula (C)**, and whose posterior end is known as the **nodulus (D)**; each hemisphere consists of an **anterior lobe (E)** which lies anterior to the **primary fissure (F)**, a flocculonodular lobe that lies rostral to the **posterolateral fissure (G)** and is composed of the nodulus (of the vermis) and the **flocculus (H)**, and a **posterior lobe (I)**, which forms the rest of the cerebellum and lies between the primary and posterolateral fissures. The cerebellum is attached to the brain stem via its peduncles: the **superior cerebellar peduncles (J)** contain primarily efferent cerebellar fibers and connect the cerebellum to the midbrain, and the **middle cerebellar peduncles (J₁)** consist of cerebellar afferent fibers and connect the cerebellum to the pons. The **inferior cerebellar peduncles (J₂)** contain cerebellar afferent and efferent fibers and connect the cerebellum to the medulla oblongata.

[Color E and F different shades of the same color; do the same for J, J₁, and J₂.]

The vermis of the cerebellum receives some of the spinocerebellar fibers and coordinates the muscle movements that are needed for walking. The flocculonodular lobe is involved in the maintenance of equilibrium and the coordination of head and eye movements.

The surface of the cerebellum is covered with gray matter and is full of convoluted gyri-like ridges known as folia, and its core is made up of white matter. The cerebellar cortex consists of three layers: (1) the outermost **molecular layer (K)**, (2) the middle **purkinje layer (L)**, and (3) the innermost **granular layer (M)**. The molecular layer consists of **basket cells (N)** and **stellate cells (O)**, both of which are interneurons that inhibit the purkinje cell. The purkinje layer consists of **purkinje cells (P)**, which send out inhibitory signals, and the granular layer is full of small cells called **granule cells (Q)** and larger cells known as **Golgi cells (R)**. Granule cells excite purkinje, basket, stellate, and golgi cells; golgi cells inhibit purkinje cells. Fibers that come from all areas except the inferior olivary nucleus enter the cerebellar cortex and terminate as **mossy fibers (S)**, and the fibers that come from the inferior olivary nucleus terminate as **climbing fibers (T)**. Mossy fibers excite granule cells, which in turn excite purkinje cells, and climbing fibers excite purkinje fibers. The climbing fiber system is involved with transmitting error signals of motor functions and the learning of new movements.

[Color K, N, and O different shades of the same color; do the same for L and P and also for M and Q.]

○ Fourth ventricle	A	○ Superior cerebellar peduncles	J	○ Purkinje cells	P
○ Vermis	B	○ Middle cerebellar peduncles	J₁	○ Granule cells	Q
○ Lingula	C	○ Inferior cerebellar peduncles	J₂	○ Golgi cells	R
○ Nodulus	D	○ Molecular layer	K	○ Mossy fibers	S
○ Anterior lobe	E	○ Purkinje layer	L	○ Climbing fibers	T
○ Primary fissure	F	○ Granular layer	M	○ Dentate nucleus	U
○ Posterolateral fissure	G	○ Basket cells	N	○ Emboliform nucleus	V
○ Flocculus	H	○ Stellate cells	O	○ Globose nucleus	W
○ Posterior lobe	I			○ Fastigial nucleus	X

Cerebellar nuclei include the following: **dentate nucleus (U)**, **emboliform nucleus (V)**, **globose nucleus (W)**, and **fastigial nucleus (X)**. These nuclei send efferent fibers to the superior and inferior cerebellar peduncles. The dentate nucleus is the largest cerebellar nucleus and contains efferent fibers that leave the nucleus to form a portion of the superior cerebellar peduncle. The globose and emboliform are collective-ly referred to as the interposed nuclei. The fastigial nucleus projects mainly to the pons and medulla and travels in the inferior cerebellar peduncle.

Clinical Correlates: *Lesions of the cerebellum may produce disturbances in balance that cause a person to lose balance and fall. This is known as ataxia.*

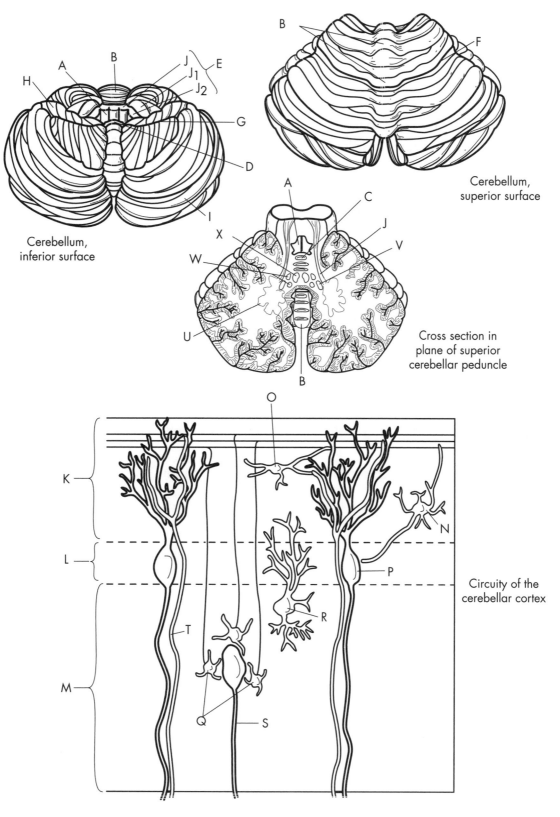

Cerebellum, inferior surface

Cerebellum, superior surface

Cross section in plane of superior cerebellar peduncle

Circuity of the cerebellar cortex

THE CEREBELLUM
self assessment

A. Middle cerebellar peduncles
B. Flocculus
C. Superior cerebellar peduncles
D. Dentate nucleus
E. Posterior lobe
F. Granular layer
G. Climbing fibers
H. Mossy fibers
I. Molecular layer
J. Inferior cerebellar peduncles
K. Globose nucleus
L. Fastigial nucleus

1. Attach cerebellum to midbrain

2. Basket and stellate cells belong to this layer of the cerebellar cortex

3. Involved with learning new movements

4. Attach cerebellum to medulla oblongata

5. Largest cerebellar nucleus

CHAPTER ELEVEN

the cerebro-vascular system

Chapter 11-1: Part I The Vertebral and Internal Carotid Arteries

Blood flows to the brain at a rate of roughly 750 ml/min and makes up about 15% of the total cardiac output. As is the case with any organ, the rate of the brain's blood supply is proportional to the rate of its metabolic activity. Since the brain is one of the most metabolically active systems in the body, it requires a fair amount of the cardiac output. The brain uses only glucose as its energy source, and so requires a steady supply of it through blood vessels; also, it cannot store the glucose and so needs to be continually supplied with it. This is why even brief interruptions in the blood supply to the brain can cause brain damage.

As the aorta emerges from the heart it becomes the **brachiocephalic trunk (A)**. The brachiocephalic trunk then divides into the **common carotid artery (B)** and the **subclavian artery (C)**. The subclavian artery then gives off a branch called the **vertebral artery (D)** that enters the foramen of the transverse processes of the sixth cervical vertebrae and pierces the dura to enter the cranium through the foramen magnum. The two vertebral arteries (one from each subclavian), give off the **posterior inferior cerebellar artery (E)**, which is a large branch that supplies the cerebellum; it also sends off branches that supply the spinal cord, these arteries are called the **anterior spinal artery (F)** and the **posterior spinal artery (G)**. The vertebral arteries join at the junction of the pons and the medulla (called the pontomedullary junction) to form the **basilar artery (H)**, which divides into right and left **posterior cerebral arteries (I)**. The posterior cerebral arteries travel around the lateral border of the midbrain and supply the occipital lobe and parts of the inferior and medial temporal lobe. As a result, the vetebrobasilar system supplies the entire brain stem, the thalami, the medial temporal lobes, and the occipital lobe.

The **internal carotid artery (J)** arises from the common carotid artery and travels through the carotid canal and cavernous sinus into the brain, where it gives off a number of branches: the opthalmic artery (not shown) supplies the eye and other orbital structures, and enters the orbit via the optic canal; the **posterior communicating artery (K)** joins the posterior cerebral artery; the **anterior choroidal artery (L)** and its branches supply the choroid plexus of the lateral ventricle, optic tract, genu of the internal capsule, and medial part of the globus pallidus. The two terminal branches of the internal carotid include the smaller **anterior cerebral artery (M)** and the larger **middle cerebral artery (N)**.

[Color all of the structures a different color.]

The anterior cerebral artery travels anteriorly in the brain, in the base of the longitudinal fissure (also called the interhemispheric fissure). Rostral to the optic chiasm, the anterior cerebral artery is joined by the **anterior communicating artery (O)**, and together they travel over the body of the corpus callosum to join the posterior cerebral artery. The anterior cerebral artery supplies the medial surface of the frontal and parietal lobes all the way to the border of the parietal-occipital sulcus.

The middle cerebral artery, which is the largest of the cerebral arteries, travels in the lateral sulcus and fans out superiorly over the frontal, parietal, and occipital lobes, and inferiorly over the temporal lobe. It sends out various branches to supply the lateral surface of the hemisphere and the claustrum, insula, caudate nucleus, lentiform nucleus, and internal capsule.

The dura mater of the brain is supplied by the meningeal arteries (not shown), the largest of which is the middle meningeal artery. The middle meningeal artery is a branch of the maxillary artery, and it alone supplies most of the dura mater.

○	Brachiocephalic trunk	A	○	Anterior spinal artery	F	○	Posterior communicating artery	K
○	Common carotid artery	B	○	Posterior spinal artery	G	○	Anterior choroidal artery	L
○	Subclavian artery	C	○	Basilar artery	H	○	Anterior cerebral artery	M
○	Vertebral artery	D	○	Posterior cerebral arteries	I	○	Middle cerebral artery	N
○	Posterior inferior cerebellar artery	E	○	Internal carotid artery	J	○	Anterior communicating artery	O

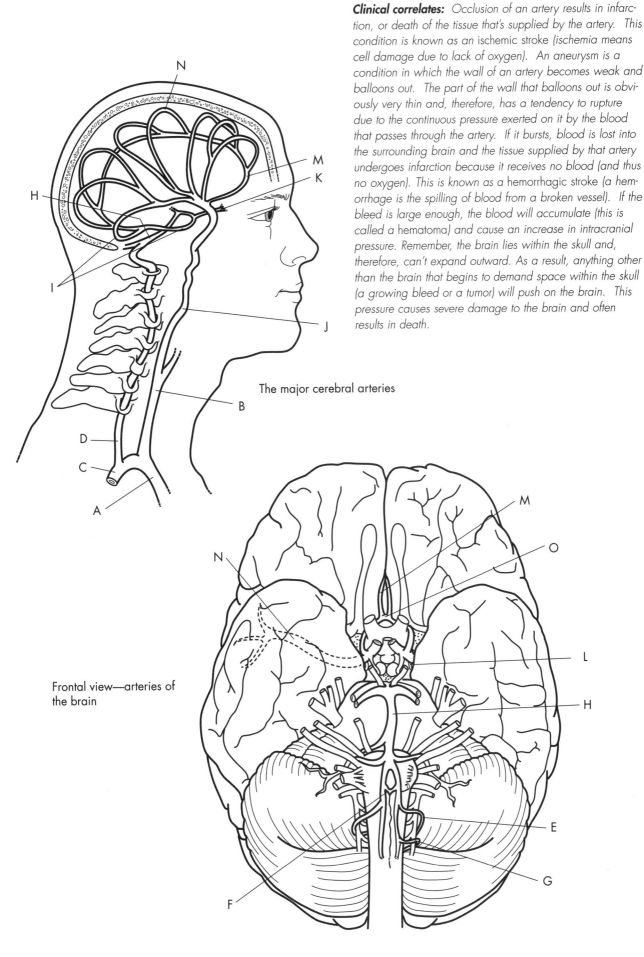

Clinical correlates: *Occlusion of an artery results in infarction, or death of the tissue that's supplied by the artery. This condition is known as an ischemic stroke (ischemia means cell damage due to lack of oxygen). An aneurysm is a condition in which the wall of an artery becomes weak and balloons out. The part of the wall that balloons out is obviously very thin and, therefore, has a tendency to rupture due to the continuous pressure exerted on it by the blood that passes through the artery. If it bursts, blood is lost into the surrounding brain and the tissue supplied by that artery undergoes infarction because it receives no blood (and thus no oxygen). This is known as a hemorrhagic stroke (a hemorrhage is the spilling of blood from a broken vessel). If the bleed is large enough, the blood will accumulate (this is called a hematoma) and cause an increase in intracranial pressure. Remember, the brain lies within the skull and, therefore, can't expand outward. As a result, anything other than the brain that begins to demand space within the skull (a growing bleed or a tumor) will push on the brain. This pressure causes severe damage to the brain and often results in death.*

The major cerebral arteries

Frontal view—arteries of the brain

-119-

Chapter 11-2: Part II The Circle of Willis, Venous Drainage, and Meningeal Arteries

Do not allow the title to this section to mislead you: the circle of Willis is not a part of the venous system, it is a part of the arterial system. The circle of Willis is the brain's attempt to provide collateral circulation in the case of arterial blockage; it also equalizes blood flow to the different parts of the brain. The circle of Willis is not the same in all people, in fact, roughly 50% of people have abnormal circle of Willis's; it has developmental variations; for example, it may be missing a crucial communicating artery.

The circle of Willis lies at the base of the brain and surrounds the optic chiasm and the tuber cinereum. It is an interlinking circular network of blood vessels made up of the following arteries: the **anterior cerebral artery (A)**, the **middle cerebral artery (B)**, the **posterior cerebral artery (C)**, the **anterior communicating artery (D)**, and the **posterior communicating artery (E)**. The anterior communicating artery is the only unpaired artery of the circle and it connects the two anterior cerebral arteries, while the posterior communicating artery connects the middle and posterior cerebral arteries.

[Color A-E different shades of red and/or pink.]

The venous drainage of the brain is routed through the dural sinuses and eventually travels into the internal jugular vein. The veins of the brain do not travel with the arteries, instead they arise through the pia mater and empty into a network of low-pressure channels known as the dural venous sinuses, which is located between the two layers of the dura mater.

The **superior sagittal sinus (F)** lies above the **falx cerebri (G)** and travels from front to back. The **inferior sagittal sinus (H)** courses superior to the corpus callosum and along the inferior border of the falx cerebri to join the **great cerebral vein (I)**; these two veins empty into the **straight sinus (J)**. The straight sinus meets the paired **transverse sinus (K)** at the occipital pole; here, the superior sagittal sinus meets these sinuses, and this area is called the **confluence of the sinuses (L)**. The transverse sinuses travel in the occipital bone and empty into the **sigmoid sinus (M)**, which in turn empties into the **internal jugular vein (N)**.

[Color F-N different shades of blue and/or purple.]

Clinical correlates: Often the communicating arteries, even if both are present, form ineffective anastomoses (linkages to another artery). This accounts for the high incidence of brain tissue damage in instances where one of the internal carotids becomes occluded. In these cases, the effects of arterial occulsion are seen in the areas of the brain that are ordinarily supplied by the occluded artery.

○ Anterior cerebral artery	A	○ Posterior communicating artery	E
○ Middle cerebral artery	B	○ Superior sagittal sinus	F
○ Posterior cerebral artery	C	○ Falx cerebri	G
○ Anterior communicating artery	D	○ Inferior sagittal sinus	H
		○ Great cerebral vein	I

○ Straight sinus	J
○ Transverse sinus	K
○ Confluence of the sinuses	L
○ Sigmoid sinus	M
○ Internal jugular vein	N

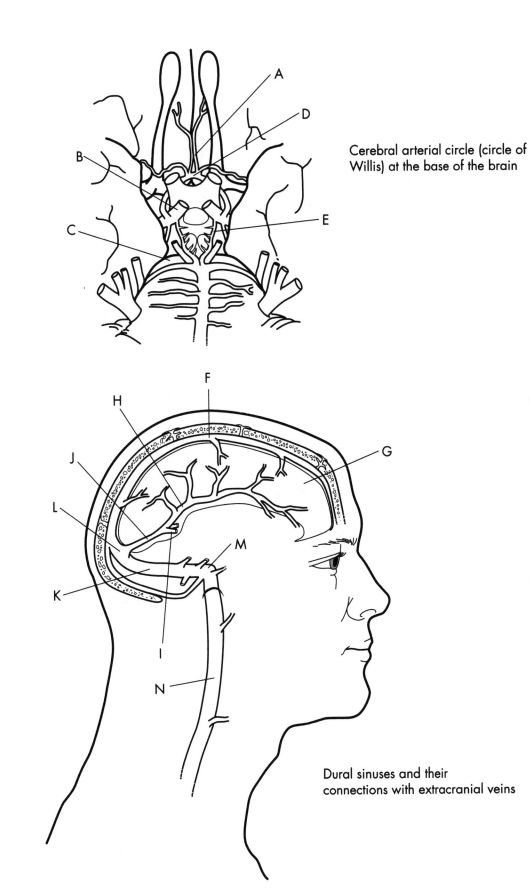

Cerebral arterial circle (circle of Willis) at the base of the brain

Dural sinuses and their connections with extracranial veins

THE CEREBROVASCULAR SYSTEM

self assessment

A. Middle cerebral artery
B. Anterior communicating artery
C. Vertebral arteries
D. Posterior communicating artery
E. Anterior cerebral artery
F. Basilar artery
G. External carotid artery
H. Posterior inferior cerebellar artery
I. Internal carotid artery
J. Transverse sinus
K. Sigmoid sinus
L. Superior sagittal sinus

1. Form the basilar artery

2. Gives off posterior cerebral arteries

3. Supplies lateral surface of cerebral hemisphere

4. Empties directly into internal jugular vein

5. Gives off ophthalmic artery

neuronal conduction

Chapter 12-1: The Resting Membrane Potential

The electrical charges on either side of the **plasma membrane (A)** of a resting nerve cell differ; there is a much higher concentration of **potassium ions (K⁺) (B)** (these are represented by triangles) inside the cell than there is outside the cell. Conversely, there is a higher concentration of **sodium ions (Na⁺) (C)** (represented by circles) outside the cell than there is inside the cell. Also contributing to the internal net negative charge are the large, negatively-charged **nondiffusible ions (D)** (represented by squares): these ions are called nondiffusible because they cannot exit the cell. The electrical charge across a nerve cell membrane at rest is –70 mV (millivolts). This means that the inside of the cell is 70 mV more negative than the outside of the cell, and this number represents the resting membrane potential (RMP). An important detail for the understanding of how nerve cells operate is that the cell membrane is almost completely impermeable to sodium but not as impermeable to potassium.

[Color all of the potassium triangles (B) one color, and then color the sodium circles (C) and nondiffusible ions (D) different colors.]

How is this ionic arrangement maintained by the cell? Well, within the cell membrane is a complex called the **sodium-potassium pump (E)**. At rest, this pump, through active transport, continuously pumps 3 Na⁺ ions out of the cell for every 2 K⁺ ions it pumps into the cell: This maintains the resting membrane potential. Since the sodium ions are more abundant outside the cell, they flow down their concentration gradient to the inside of the cell. Also, since the inside of the cell is negative and sodium ions are positive—and because opposite charges attract—the sodium ions are pulled to the cell interior via an electrical gradient. So it is appropriate to say that two gradients, concentration and electrical, pull the sodium to the cell's interior. Since potassium ions are in abundance inside the cell, their concentration gradient pulls them out of the cell. However, since they are positively charged and since the outside of the cell is positive, their electrical gradient serves to keep them inside the cell. So unlike the gradients for sodium, the two gradients for potassium pull the ions in opposite directions.

[Color A-E different colors.]

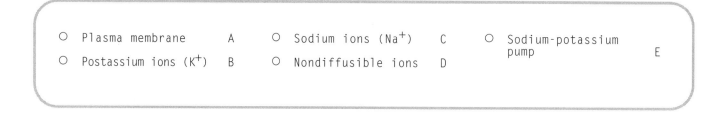

○ Plasma membrane   A   ○ Sodium ions (Na⁺)   C   ○ Sodium-potassium pump   E

○ Postassium ions (K⁺)   B   ○ Nondiffusible ions   D

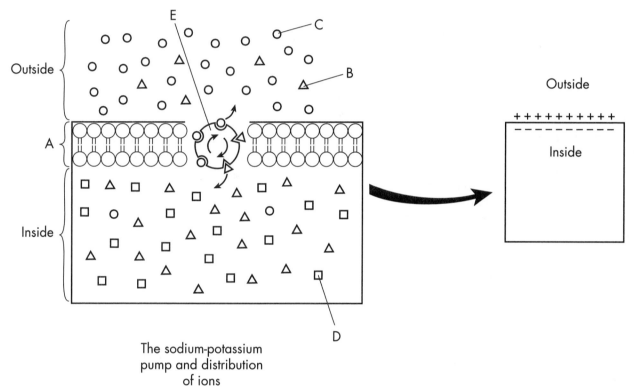

The sodium-potassium
pump and distribution
of ions

Chapter 12-2: The Action Potential, Synapse, and Neuromuscular Junction

The following discussion will outline two types of neuronal communication: neuron to neuron communication, and neuron to muscle communication. The former takes place at the synapse and the latter occurs at the neuromuscular junction. Let's discuss the synapse first.

The structure of a neuron includes a **cell body (A)**, an **axon (B)**, which is involved in the propogation of action potentials, and **dendrites (C)**, which are extensions of the cell body that receive information. The axon is wrapped in short segments of what is called a **myelin sheath (D)**; the small myelin-less segments are known as **nodes of Ranvier (D$_1$)**. The neural signal jumps from node to node in a process called saltatory conduction; this type of transmission is much faster than if the action potential had travelled the entire length of the axon.

The **presynaptic terminal (E)** of one neuron synapses with the cell body of a **postsynaptic neuron (F)**. The terminal of the postsynaptic neuron is therefore called the postsynaptic terminal.

[Color A, B, and C different shades of the same color. Color D yellow and D$_1$ black.]

Embedded in the cell membrane are voltage-gated channels for sodium and potassium. Sodium has both an activation gate and an inactivation gate, while potassium has only one gate that acts as the activation and inactivation gate. When a stimulus of sufficient strength reaches the cell membrane, it causes a conformational change in the voltage-gated channel, causing it to open. This results in a large influx of sodium into the cell, which changes the value of the membrane potential to +20 mV. Immediately following this event, the sodium inactivation gate closes to prevent further influx of sodium ions. This entire process is known as depolarization.

Shortly after the sodium activation gate opens, the potassium gate begins to open slowly, allowing potassium to begin exiting the cell. This process is known as repolarization, an event that restores the resting membrane potential. The potassium gate remains open for a short time after repolarization is complete, and the membrane potential reaches a value of −100 mV before returning to the −70 mV.

Inside the neuron are **transmitter vesicles (G)** that contain neurotransmitters (for example, GABA, serotonin, and norepinephrine). Neurotransmitters are chemical messangers that allow communication between neurons. When a neuron is in the depolarized state, a calcium influx into the cell causes fusion of the neurotransmitter-containing vesicles to the presynaptic membrane. Generally, each neuron secretes one type of neurotransmitter. These neurotransmitters travel across the **synaptic cleft (H)** (in one direction only), which is the space between the presynaptic and postsynaptic neurons, to associate with **receptor proteins (I)** on the postsynaptic neuron's membrane. The change that these neurotransmitters induce depends upon the neurotransmitter released (some are excitatory while others are inhibitory), and its interaction with a specific postsynaptic receptor protein. For instance, if the interaction is an excitatory one, the postsynaptic membrane will undergo depolarization and the process continues through a series of neurons. The degree of change in the membrane potential of the postsynaptic membrane is proportional to the amount of neurotransmitter released. Neurotransmitters such as norepinephrine are removed from the synaptic cleft through reuptake (that is, they are endocytocized into the presynaptic neuron from the synapse.

[Color E–I different colors.]

The neuromuscular junction utilizes essentially the same mechanism as the one we just described, but the junction is outside the central nervous system, since it involves skeletal muscles, and the principal neurotransmitter is acetylcholine (ACh). This is an excitatory interaction with the postsynaptic receptor, and the

---

○ Cell body	A	○ Myelin sheath	D	○ Transmitter vesicles	G
○ Axon	B	○ Nodes of Ranvier	D$_1$	○ Synaptic cleft	H
○ Dendrites	C	○ Presynaptic terminal	E	○ Receptor proteins	I
		○ Postsynaptic neuron	F		

result is muscle contraction. Rather than returning to the presynaptic neuron, ACh is removed from the synaptic cleft by an enzyme known as acetylcholinesterase (AChE).

Clinical Correlates: *There exists a condition in which antibodies destroy acetylcholine receptors on skeletal muscles. As a result, ACh cannot depolarize the skeletal muscle membranes and, therefore, the muscle cannot contract. This disease is known as myasthenia gravis.*

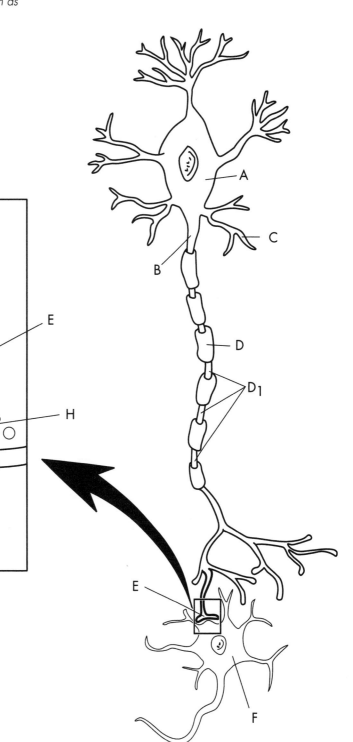

The synapse

the autonomic nervous system

Chapter 13-1: The Autonomic Nervous System Part I

The nervous system is divided into somatic and autonomic segments. The somatic nervous system (SNS) regulates the voluntary activity of skeletal muscles, and the autonomic nervous system (ANS) regulates the involuntary activities of smooth muscle, cardiac muscle, and glands; these are collectively called the **effectors (A)**. Put another way, the ANS, which is an almost purely motor system, sends out visceral efferent fibers that supply the viscera. Viscera are essentially internal organs contained within a cavity, such as the abdominal organs. Some examples of the visceral activities of the ANS include: increasing and decreasing the heart rate, constricting and dilating the pupils, and increasing the motility of the gastrointestinal tract. The ANS is controlled by the cerebral cortex, the hypothalamus, and the medulla.

Motor fibers of the SNS travel from the CNS to synapse directly with skeletal muscle. The motor system of the ANS, on the other hand, involves a 2-neuron system; a preganglionic neuron and a postganglionic neuron. The cell body of the preganglionic neuron lies in the brain or spinal cord, and the cell body of the postganglionic neuron lies in an **autonomic ganglion (B)**, which is outside the CNS. In addition, the neurotransmitter used by the SNS is acetylcholine (ACh), which causes excitation of its effector, while the neurotransmitters used by the ANS are norepinephrine (NE) and ACh, and they may inhibit or excite the effector, depending upon the neurotransmitter, the organ, and the particular division of the ANS. The axon of the preganglionic neuron is myelinated and is called a **preganglionic fiber (C)**. This preganglionic fiber carries impulses from the CNS to an autonomic ganglion, where it synapses with the **cell body of the postganglionic neuron (D)**. The axon of the postganglionic neuron is unmyelinated and is called a **postganglionic fiber (E)**; it carries impulses from the autonomic ganglion to the effector organ. In the autonomic ganglion, the preganglionic fiber synapses with several postganglionic fibers at one time. These postganglionic fibers then pass to various effector organs.

[Color A-E different colors.]

There are two divisions of the ANS: the sympathetic division and the parasympathetic division. Both systems have preganglionic and postganglionic neuron systems. The autonomic ganglia of the sympathetic division are located close to the spinal cord, but their effector organs are located far from the ganglia. Therefore, sympathetic preganglionic fibers tend to be short—since they do not have far to travel from their cell body in the spinal cord to the nearby autonomic ganglion—and sympathetic postganglionic fibers tend to be long. Conversely, the autonomic ganglia of the parasympathetic system are located far from the spinal cord and close to the effector organ (sometimes even within the walls of the effector organ). As a result of this, parasympathetic preganglionic fibers tend to be long and parasympathetic postganglionic fibers tend to be short.

The sympathetic division has two different types of ganglia: the **sympathetic trunk ganglion (F)** and the **prevertebral ganglion (G)**; the former are arranged in vertical rows on each side of the spinal column, and the latter lie anterior to the spinal column. The sympathetic preganglionic fibers have their cell bodies in the **lateral gray horn (H)** of spinal cord segments T1 to L3 (first thoracic to third lumbar). The sympathetic preganglionic fibers leave the spinal cord through the **ventral root (I)** of a spinal nerve, through the **white ramus communicans (J)**, and finally through the **sympathetic trunk (K)** from which they travel to either a sympathetic trunk ganglion or a prevertebral ganglion. The **gray ramus communicans (L)** connect the sympathetic trunk ganglion to the spinal nerve. The postganglionic fibers then travel to their respective visceral receptors.

[Color F–I different colors.]

○	Effectors	A	○	Postganglionic fiber	E
○	Autonomic ganglion	B	○	Sympathetic trunk ganglion	F
○	Preganglionic fiber	C	○	Prevertebral ganglion	G
○	Cell body of the postganglionic neuron	D	○	Lateral gray horn	H

○	Ventral root	I
○	White ramus communicans	J
○	Sympathetic trunk	K
○	Gray ramus communicans	L

Preganglionic and postganglionic neurons of the sympathetic system

A
Smooth muscle
Cardiac muscle
Glands

Ganglia of the sympathetic division of the autonomic nervous system

Chapter 13-2: The Autonomic Nervous System Part II

The synapses of the autonomic nervous system function by way of neurotransmitters. The autonomic fibers that use acetylcholine (ACh) as their primary neurotransmitter are known as cholinergic fibers, and those that use norepinephrine (NE) are called adrenergic fibers. All preganglionic fibers (sympathetic and parasympathetic) are cholinergic fibers, and all parasympathetic postganglionic fibers are also cholinergic. In general, most of the postganglionic sympathetic fibers are adrenergic, excepting the following cholinergic fibers: fibers that travel to the piloerector muscles, the sweat glands, and a few blood vessels.

[Color the parasympathetic fibers one color and the sympathetic fibers another color.]

[Color the ganglia of the parasympathetic side a different shade of the color used for the parasympathetic fibers; do the same for the sympathetic ganglia.]

ACh and NE both act on specific receptors. ACh has two types of receptors: nicotinic receptors and muscarinic receptors. You may recall that in the action potential chapter, the membrane of the postsynaptic neuron had receptor proteins on it that were acted upon by the neurotransmitter that was released by the presynaptic neuron. These receptor proteins are exactly the ones that we are now discussing. Muscarinic receptors are found in the effectors that are innervated by all parasympathetic postganglionic fibers and sympathetic cholinergic postganglionic fibers. Nicotinic receptors are found in the following locations: (1) in every synapse between a preganglionic fiber and postganglionic fiber (sympathetic and parasympathetic); in other words they lie in all autonomic ganglia, and (2) in skeletal muscle fibers of the neuromuscular junction.

NE also binds to two types of receptors: alpha (α) receptors and beta (β) receptors. Alpha receptors are further subdivided into alpha$_1$ (α_1), alpha$_2$ (α_2), beta$_1$ (β_1), beta$_2$ (β_2). In general, the effect that a particular neurotransmitter has on an effector depends largely upon the receptor that's being acted upon. Therefore, one neurotransmitter that acts upon two different receptors will often produce two different results. Alpha$_1$ receptors predominate in salivary glands and smooth muscle, where they stimulate the secretion of salivary glands and promote the contraction of arterioles, bronchioles, the bladder, and the uterus. Alpha$_2$ receptors promote mast cell (cells that are involved with the immune system) degranulation, the release of insulin, and facilitate the reuptake of NE from the synaptic cleft. Beta$_1$ receptors increase the heart rate, and beta$_2$ receptors cause dilation of the bronchials.

Parasympathetic

Sympathetic

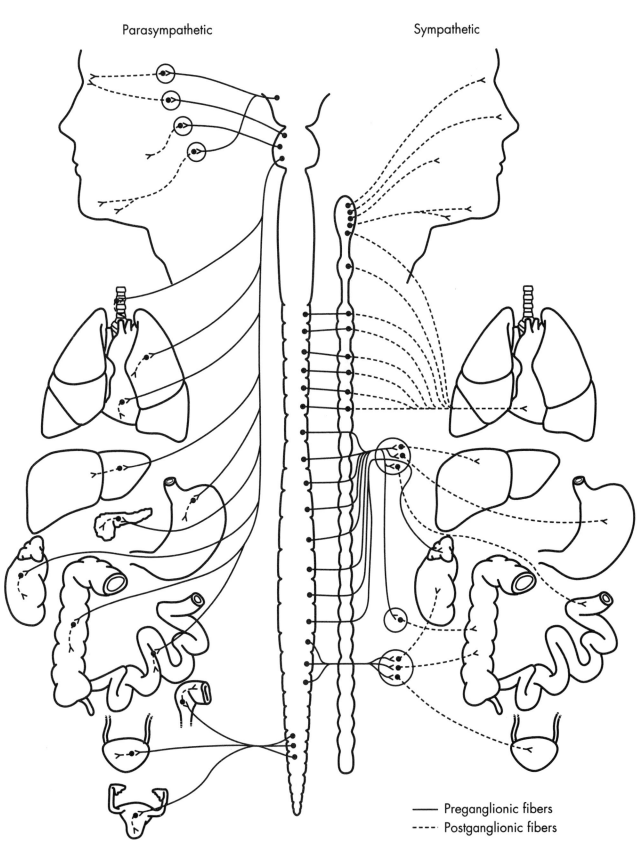

—— Preganglionic fibers
----- Postganglionic fibers

CHAPTER FOURTEEN

ascending neuronal pathways

Chapter 14-1: Lateral Spinothalamic Pathway

Now we will discuss the sensory pathways. Upon entering the spinal cord, sensory nerve fibers are organized into neuronal tracts. Some of the tracts link different spinal cord segments, while others ascend into the brain. The **first-order neuron (A)** finds its cell body outside the central nervous system, in the dorsal root ganglion of the spinal nerve. The axons of this cell body divide into both a central and peripheral branch, and the central branch enters the spinal cord or brain by way of a dorsal (sensory) root, while the peripheral branch innervates organs by way of a sensory nerve. The localized area of skin that is innervated by a dorsal (sensory) root is known as a dermatome.

The **second-order neuron (B)** has its cell body in the dorsal horn of the spinal cord or medullary relay nuclei; its axons then decussate (cross) the midline to ascend through higher levels of the CNS. These ascending fibers run in the white matter of the spinal cord and are called tracts.

The **third-order neuron (C)** has its cell body in the thalamic relay nuclei. Its axons then travel to the somatosensory cortex.

The **lateral spinothalamic tract (D)** conveys information about pain, temperature, and crude touch. The axon of the first-order neuron synapses with the cell body of the second-order neuron in the posterior gray horn of the spinal cord. The axon of the second-order neuron then crosses to the opposite side of the spinal cord in the ventral white commissure and ascends in the lateral white column. The tract ascends through the brainstem

and joins the medial lemniscus to synapse with third-order neurons located in the **ventral posterolateral nucleus of the thalamus (E)** (Note that a tract of sensory fibers in the medulla or pons is often referred to as a lemniscus). The axons of the third-order neuron then transmit sensory impulses through the **internal capsule (F)** to the **somatosensory cortex (G)**. Through this arrangement, the lateral spinothalamic tract conveys information about pain, temperature, and crude touch from the opposite upper and lower extremities. Incidentally, an easy way to tell whether a tract is ascending or descending is simply to look at its name. For instance, the spinothalamic goes from the spine to the thalamus, and fibers going toward the brain are afferent, or sensory, therefore, this must be an ascending (sensory) tract.

[Color A-G different colors.]

Clinical Correlates: *Damage to the spinothalamic tract that results from a lesion in the spinal cord will cause a contralateral loss of pain and temperature sensation. Remember that the second-order neuron crosses to the opposite side of the spinal cord.*

○ First-order neuron   A

○ Second-order neuron   B

○ Third-order neuron   C

○ Lateral spinothalamic tract   D

○ Ventral posterolateral nucleus of the thalamus   E

○ Internal capsule   F

○ Somatosensory cortex   G

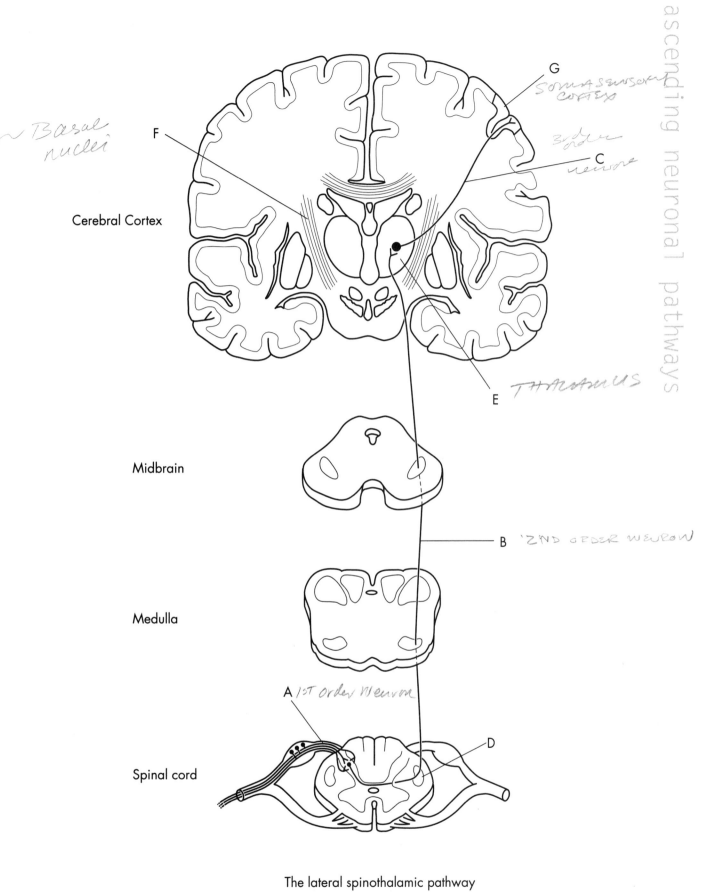

~Basal nuclei

Cerebral Cortex

G SOMASENSORY CORTEX

3rd order neuron

C

F

E THALAMUS

Midbrain

B '2ND ORDER NEURON

Medulla

A 1ST Order Neuron

Spinal cord

D

The lateral spinothalamic pathway

SENSORY

Chapter 14-2: Dorsal Column and Spinocerebellar Pathways

This tract is also called the dorsal column-medial lemniscal pathway or the posterior column pathway. It is named as such because it travels in the dorsal column of the spinal cord, then to the thalamus by way of the medial lemniscus, which is a cerebral white matter tract that passes through the medulla, pons, and midbrain. The posterior column pathway mediates fine touch, proprioception (position sense), and vibratory sensation.

Axons of the **first-order neuron (A)** of this pathway travel up the **dorsal white column (B)** of the spinal cord as the **fasciculus gracilis (C)** and **fasciculus cuneatus (D)**. The fasciculus gracilis is located medially and the fasciculus cuneatus lies laterally; the former carries sensory information from the lower extremities and lower trunk, while the latter carries sensory information from the upper extremities and upper trunk. The axon of the first-order neuron enters the medulla and synapses with the cell body of the **second-order neuron (E)** in either the **nucleus gracilis (F)** or **nucleus cuneatus (G)**. The axon of the second-order neuron becomes one of the internal arcuate fibers, crosses to the other side of the lower medulla, and ascends in the **medial lemniscus (H)** to synapse with the cellbody of the **third-order neuron (I)** in the **ventral posteromedial nucleus of the thalamus (J)**. The axons of the third-order neuron then travel through the **internal capsule (K)** to reach the **somatosensory cortex (L)**.

Another set of ascending tracts also exist, and they will be discussed briefly here. These ascending tracts are the spinocerebellar pathways. The anterior spinocerebellar tract enters the spinal cord at lumbar and sacral levels and synapses with second-order neurons; the majority of these fibers cross over and ascend to the cerebellum on the opposite side, entering it through the superior cerebellar peduncle. This tract conveys information from muscles and joints about movement and position sense. The posterior spinocerebellar tract enters the spinal cord, synapses with second-order neurons that ascend in the lateral white column of the spinal cord to the medulla, and then travels to the cerebellum and enters via the inferior cerebellar peduncle. It also conveys information about muscle position and movement to the cerebellum, so that the cerebellum may, in turn, help coordinate fine motor control and the precise movement of these muscles.

Clinical Correlates: *Damage to the dorsal column pathway results in a loss of position and vibratory sense below the level of the lesion.*

○ First-order neuron	A	○ Second-order neuron	E	○ Ventral posteromedial nucleus of the thalamus	J
○ Dorsal white column	B	○ Nucleus gracilis	F		
○ Fasciculus gracilis	C	○ Nucleus cuneatus	G	○ Internal capsule	K
○ Fasciculus cuneatus	D	○ Medial lemniscus	H	○ Somatosensory cortex	L
		○ Third-order neuron	I		

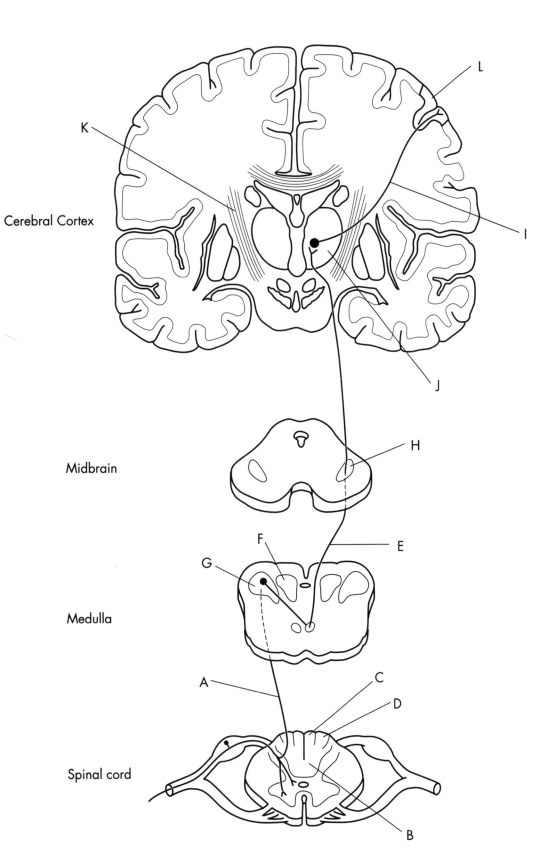

Cerebral Cortex

Midbrain

Medulla

Spinal cord

The dorsal column pathway

CHAPTER FIFTEEN

descending neuronal pathways

Chapter 15-1: Corticospinal Pathway

As you can see in the art on the right, there exists both a **lateral corticospinal tract (A)** and an **anterior corticospinal tract (B)**; these pathways are also commonly referred to as the pyramidal tracts.

[Color A and B different shades of the same color.]

The corticospinal tract arises mainly from the motor cortices, but a smaller portion of this tract arises from the somatosensory cortex. It leaves the cortex to travel through the posterior limb of the **internal capsule (C)**, the **cerebral peduncles (D)**, and the brain stem, and then forms the pyramids of the medulla oblongota. The majority of fibers then decussate in the medulla and descend in the spinal cord as the lateral corticospinal tract. The fibers terminate in the **anterior gray horn (E)** of the spinal cord and synapse with association neurons, which in turn synapse with lower motor neurons. This conglomerate leaves the spinal cord through the ventral roots of the spinal nerve and innervates skeletal muscles. Since the fibers cross in the medulla, the motor cortex of one side of the brain controls movement on the opposite side of the body.

[Color C–E different colors.]

The remaining fibers do not cross and simply descend in the anterior white column of the spinal cord as the anterior corticospinal tract. These fibers cross over later in the spinal cord.

Another segment of the pyramidal pathway is the corticobulbar tract (not shown), which is involved with the movement of the head and neck. It leaves the motor cortex and travels to the brain stem with the corticospinal tracts. Here they cross and terminate in the nuclei of all the cranial nerves except cranial nerves I, II, and VIII.

Clinical Correlates: *Damage to the corticospinal tract would result in muscle weakness or paralysis.*

○ Lateral corticospinal tract	A	○ Cerebral peduncles	D
○ Anterior corticospinal tract	B	○ Anterior gray horn	E
○ Internal capsule	C		

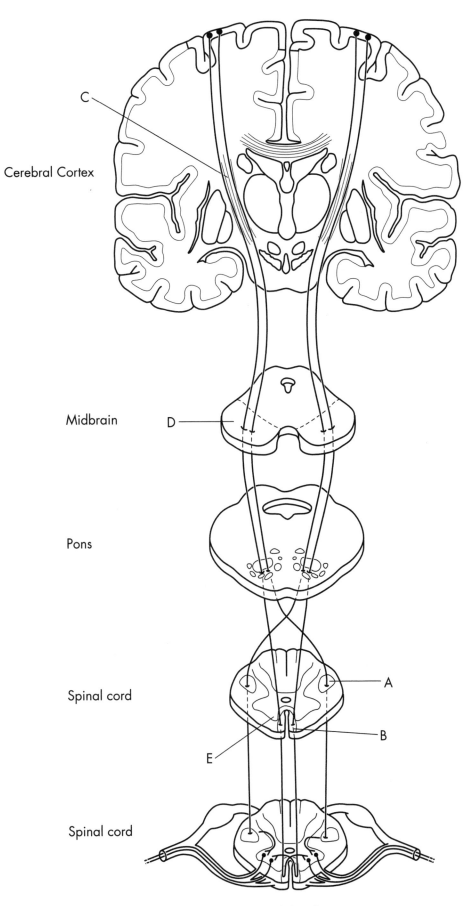

Cerebral Cortex

C

Midbrain

D

Pons

Spinal cord

A

B

E

Spinal cord

Pyramidal pathways

Chapter 15-2: Rubrospinal and Tectospinal

The **rubrospinal tract (A)** is an indirect pathway involved with the control of arm flexor muscles on the contralateral side; it arises from the **red nucleus (B)** of the midbrain and spans the length of the spinal cord. From the red nucleus the tract crosses in the ventral tegmental decussation (not shown) and descends in the lateral white column of the spinal cord, abutting fibers of the lateral corticospinal tract. The fibers of this tract terminate in the anterior horn of the spinal cord segments, synapsing with other neurons known as internuncial neurons.

[Color B red and color A a lighter shade of red.]

The **tectospinal tract (C)** is thought to be involved with reflex movements of the head that occur in response to visual stimuli. This tract arises from the **superior colliculus (D)** of the midbrain and crosses in the dorsal tegmental decussation (not shown). It descends in the brain stem, close to the medial longitudinal fasciculus (MLF) (not shown), then descends in the spinal cord in the anterior white commissure. The tract terminates in the anterior horn of the cervical segments of the spinal cord; it does not extend beyond the cervical segments. It is fitting that this tract arises from the superior colliculus and travels close to the MLF because the superior colliculus sends signals via the MLF to turn the head in response to a visual stimulus.

[Color C and D different shades of the same color.]

Clinical Correlates: *Destruction of the rubrospinal tract impairs movements of the hands and fingers.*

○ Rubrospinal tract   A   ○ Tectospinal tract   C

○ Red nucleus   B   ○ Superior colliculus   D

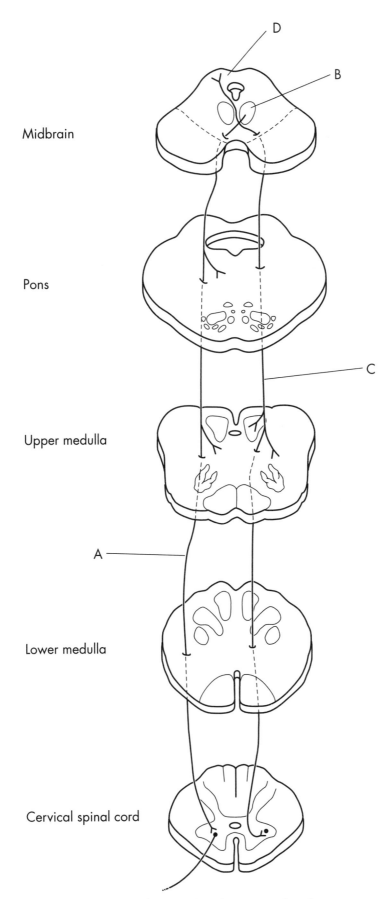

D

B

Midbrain

Pons

C

Upper medulla

A

Lower medulla

Cervical spinal cord

Rubrospinal and tectospinal pathways

Chapter 15-3: Reticulospinal and Vestibulospinal Pathways

We will discuss these two tracts together, since they both arise from the pons, and because their functions are somewhat related.

The reticulospinal system is involved in reflexive and voluntary movement. There are two reticulospinal tracts that come from different nuclei: (1) the **pontine reticulospinal tract (A)** comes from pontine reticular nuclei, and (2) the **medullary reticulospinal tract (B)** comes from medullary reticular nuclei. The nuclei work against each other; the pontine nuclei excite the antigravity muscles (the muscles of the spine, the flexors of upper limbs, and the extensors of lower limbs) and the medullary nuclei inhibit them. The **lateral vestibulospinal tract (C)** arises from the **lateral vestibular nucleus (D)**. The vestibular nuclei work in concert with the pontine reticular nuclei in exciting the antigravity muscles. The vestibular nuclei are involved in the maintenance of equilibrium and balance; they use the information they receive from the vestibular apparatus of the inner ear to regulate the excitation of the antigravity muscles in order to achieve balance.

[Color A and B different colors. Color C and D different shades of the same color.]

The pontine reticulospinal tract (or medial reticulospinal tract) arises from the pontine reticular nuclei and descends in the spinal cord (without crossing) in the anterior funiculus. It spans the length of the spinal cord and terminates in the anterior horn, and then it goes on to innervate extensor muscles of the spine and limbs.

The medullary reticulospinal tract (or lateral reticulospinal tract) arises from the medullary reticular nuclei. Most fibers of this tract do not cross, but descend in the lateral white column and travel the full length of the spinal cord. They terminate in the anterior horn and serve to inhibit the extensor reflexes of the spinal and limb muscles.

The lateral vestibulospinal tract arises from the lateral vestibul-ar nucleus and travels down the spinal cord (without crossing) in the anterior white column. It terminates primarily in the anterior horns of the spinal cord's cervical and lumbar segments.

Clinical Correlates: *Damage to these descending pathways may result in impairments of balance, posture, and equilibrium.*

○ Pontine reticulospinal tract   A   ○ Lateral vestibulospinal tract   C

○ Medullary reticulospinal tract   B   ○ Lateral vestibular nucleus   D

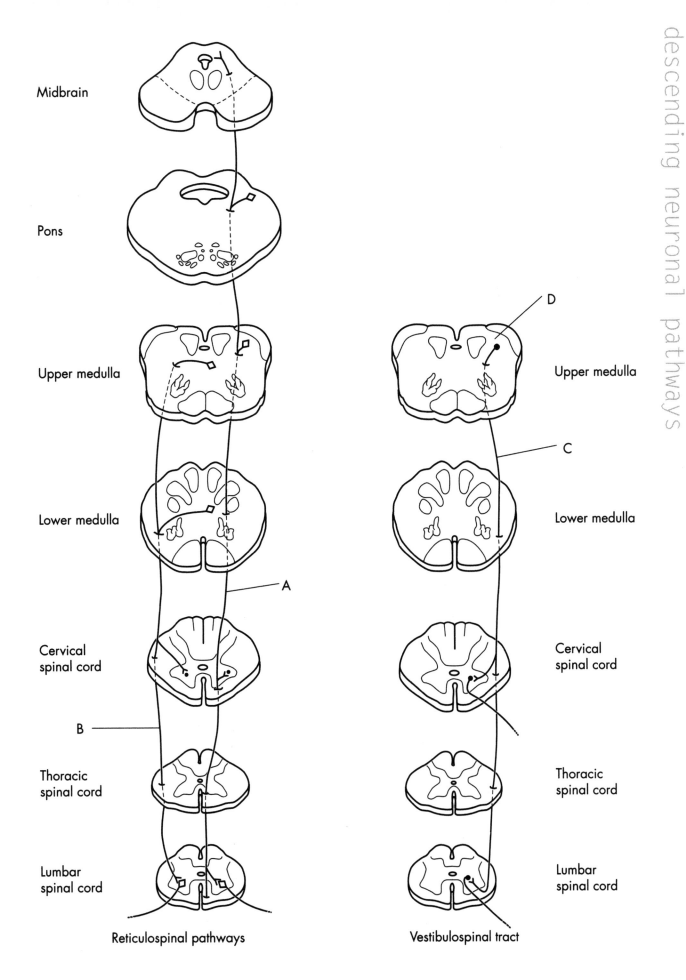

Midbrain

Pons

Upper medulla

D

Upper medulla

C

Lower medulla

Lower medulla

A

Cervical
spinal cord

Cervical
spinal cord

B

Thoracic
spinal cord

Thoracic
spinal cord

Lumbar
spinal cord

Lumbar
spinal cord

Reticulospinal pathways

Vestibulospinal tract

CHAPTER SIXTEEN

the human brain atlas

surfaces of the brain

Chapter 16-1: Lateral Surface of the Brain

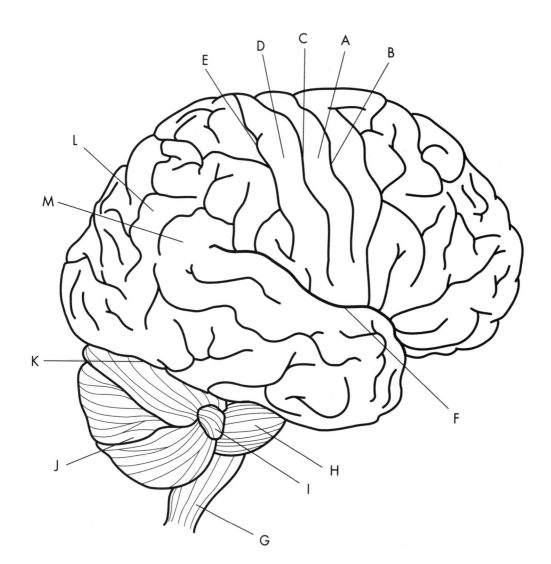

○ Precentral gyrus	A	○ Postcentral sulcus	E	○ Cerebellar hemisphere J
○ Precentral sulcus	B	○ Lateral sulcus	F	○ Preoccipital notch K
○ Central sulcus	C	○ Medulla	G	○ Angular gyrus L
○ Postcentral gyrus	D	○ Pons	H	○ Supramarginal gyrus M
		○ Flocculus	I	

Chapter 16-2: Inferior Surface of the Brain

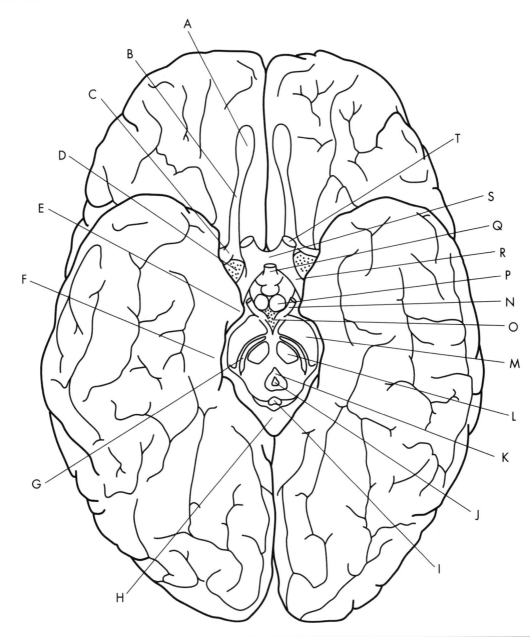

○ Olfactory bulb	A	○ Splenium of corpus callosum	H	○ Oculomotor nerve (CN III)	N
○ Olfactory tract	B	○ Pineal gland	I	○ Posterior perforated substance	O
○ Lateral olfactory stria	C	○ Cerebral aqueduct	J	○ Mammillary body	P
○ Anterior perforated substance	D	○ Periaqueductal gray matter	K	○ Infundibulum	Q
○ Uncus	E	○ Red nucleus	L	○ Optic tract	R
○ Parahippocampal gyrus	F	○ Basis pedunculi	M	○ Optic chiasm	S
○ Substantia nigra	G			○ Optic nerve (CN II)	T

Chapter 16-3: Superior Surface of the Brain

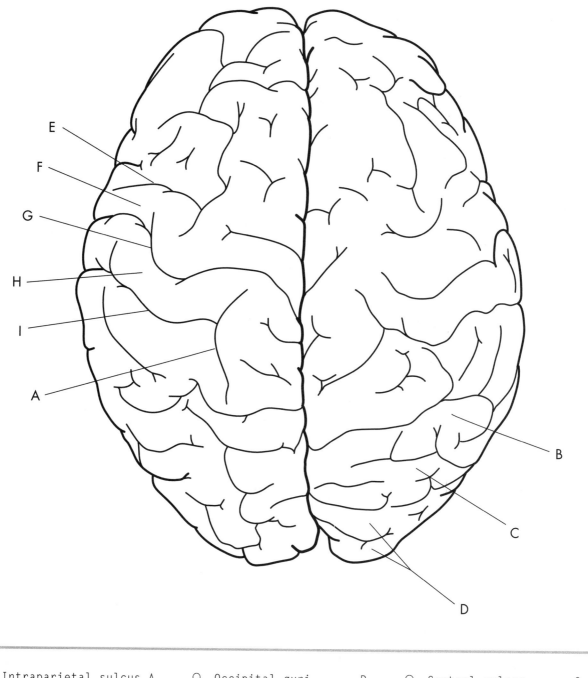

○ Intraparietal sulcus	A	○ Occipital gyri	D	○ Central sulcus	G
○ Supramarginal gyrus	B	○ Precentral sulcus	E	○ Postcentral gyrus	H
○ Angular gyrus	C	○ Precentral gyrus	F	○ Postcentral sulcus	I

CHAPTER SEVENTEEN

the human brain atlas

serial coronal sections

Following is a series of coronal sections cut in series in an anterior to posterior direction. That is, each successive diagram will illustrate a section posterior to the one before it.

Chapter 17-1: Section through Frontal Lobes

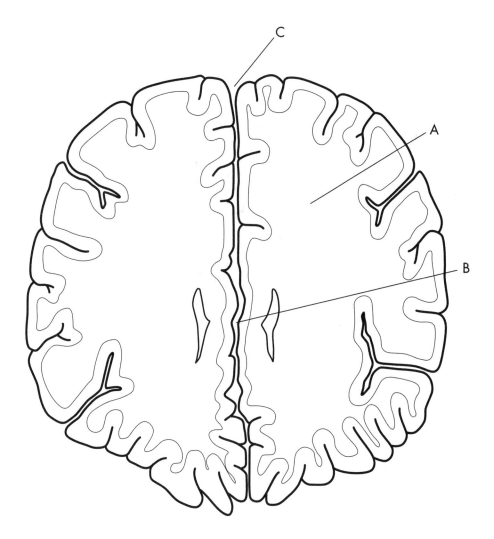

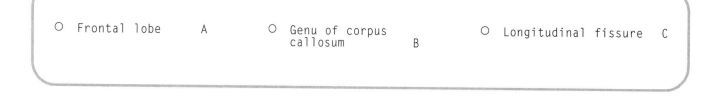

○ Frontal lobe   A   ○ Genu of corpus callosum   B   ○ Longitudinal fissure   C

Chapter 17-2: Section through Temporal Horns of Lateral Ventricles

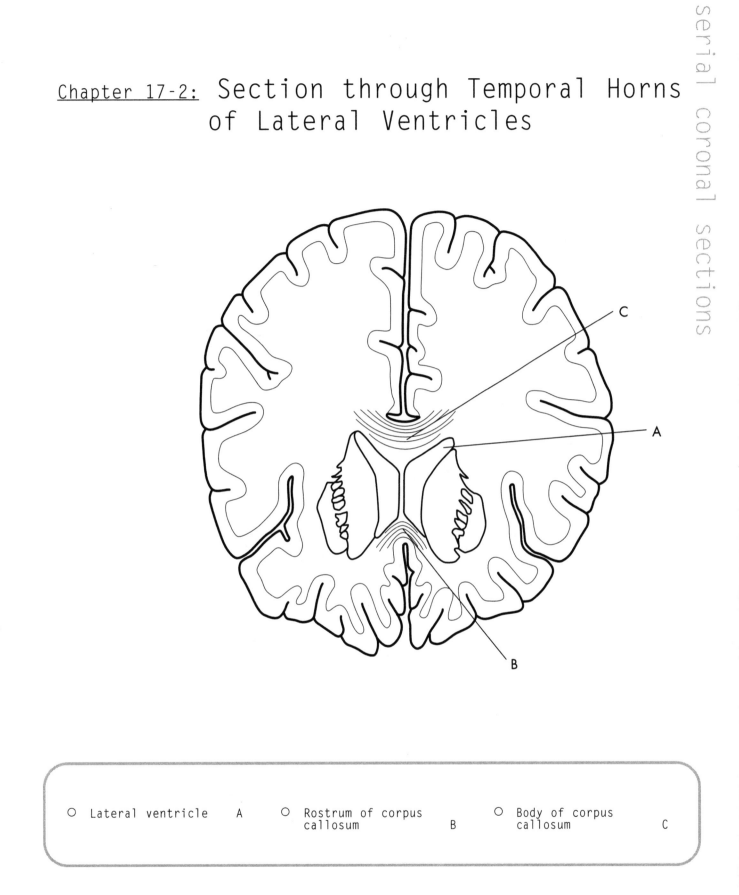

○ Lateral ventricle	A	○ Rostrum of corpus callosum	B	○ Body of corpus callosum	C

CHAPTER SEVENTEEN

Chapter 17-3: Section through Anterior Commissure

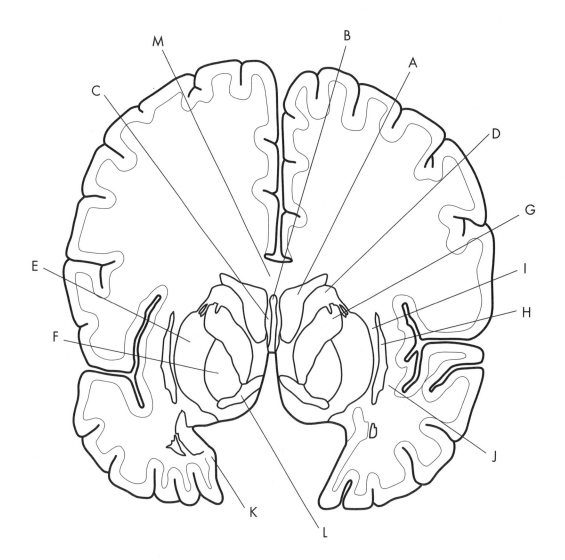

○ Anterior horn of
   lateral ventricle   A

○ Septum pellucidum   B

○ Column of fornix   C

○ Head of caudate
   nucleus   D

○ Putamen   E

○ Globus pallidus   F

○ Anterior limb of
   internal capsule   G

○ Claustrum   H

○ External capsule   I

○ Extreme capsule   J

○ Uncus   K

○ Anterior commissure   L

○ Body of corpus
   callosum   M

Chapter 17-4: Section through Body of Lateral Ventricles at the Level of the Superior Colliculus

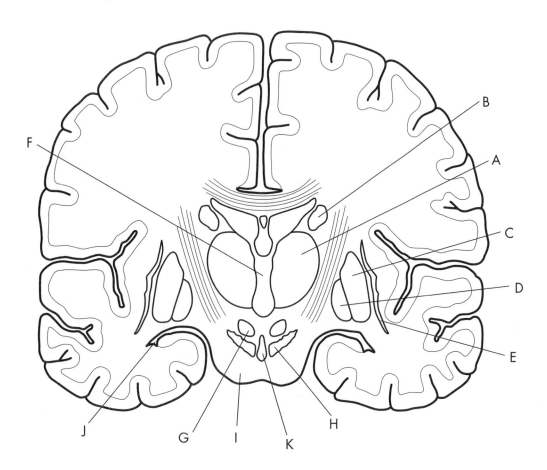

○ Thalamus	A	○ Globus pallidus	D	○ Substantia nigra	H	
○ Body of caudate nucleus	B	○ Claustrum	E	○ Superior colliculus	I	
○ Putamen	C	○ Third ventricle	F	○ Inferior horn of lateral ventricle	J	
		○ Red nucleus	G	○ Cerebral aqueduct	K	

Chapter 17-5: Section through the Posterior Horns of Lateral Ventricles

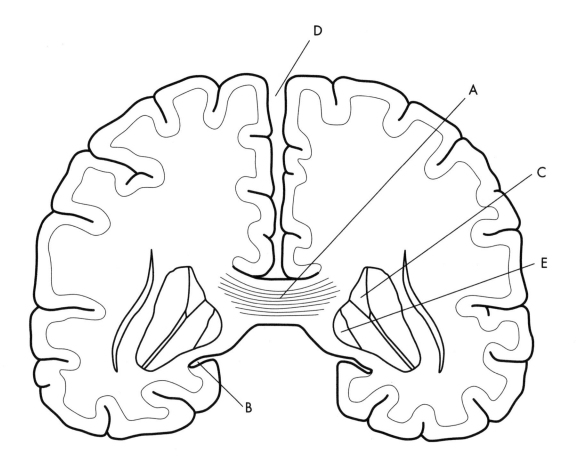

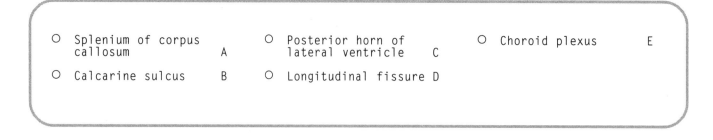

○ Splenium of corpus
  callosum   A

○ Calcarine sulcus   B

○ Posterior horn of
  lateral ventricle   C

○ Longitudinal fissure D

○ Choroid plexus   E

Chapter 17-6: Section through Pons

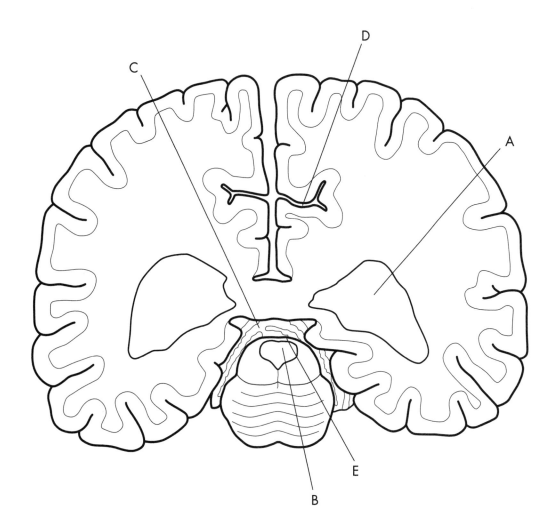

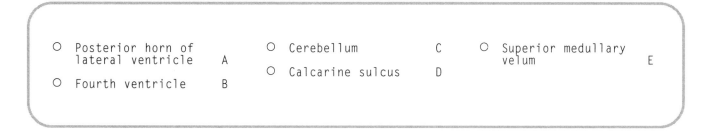

○ Posterior horn of
  lateral ventricle   A

○ Fourth ventricle   B

○ Cerebellum   C

○ Calcarine sulcus   D

○ Superior medullary
  velum   E

CHAPTER EIGHTEEN

the human brain atlas

serial sagittal sections of the cerebral hemisphere

Following is a series of sagittal sections. Each successive section is more lateral than the previous one.

Chapter 18-1: Midsagittal Section of Cerebral Hemisphere

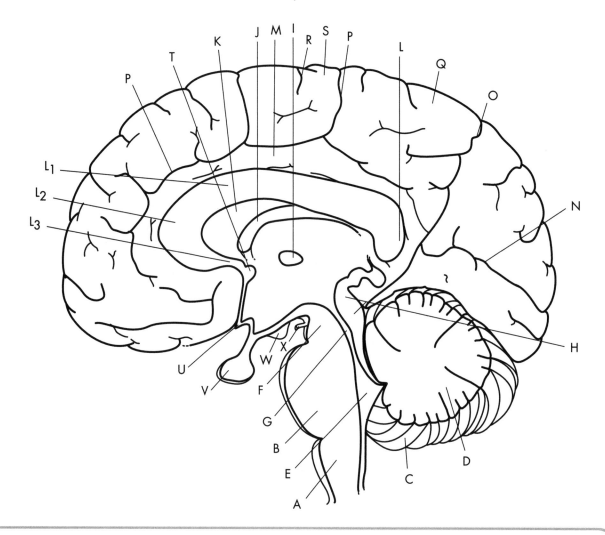

○ Medulla	A	○ Fornix	J	○ Parieto-occipital sulcus	O
○ Pons	B	○ Septum pellucidum	K	○ Cingulate sulcus	P
○ Cerebellar hemisphere	C	○ Splenium of corpus callosum	L	○ Postcentral gyrus	Q
○ Vermis of cerebellum	D			○ Central sulcus	R
○ Fourth ventricle	E	○ Body of corpus callosum	L₁	○ Precentral gyrus	S
○ Midbrain	F	○ Genu of corpus callosum	L₂	○ Anterior commissure	T
○ Cerebral aqueduct	G			○ Optic chiasm	U
○ Superior and inferior colliculi	H	○ Rostrum of corpus callosum	L₃	○ Pituitary gland	V
		○ Cingulate gyrus	M	○ Mammillary body	W
○ Interthalamic adhesion (Massa intermedia)	I	○ Calcarine fissure	N	○ Oculomotor nerve (CN III)	X

Chapter 18-2: Section through Anterior Thalamic Nucleus

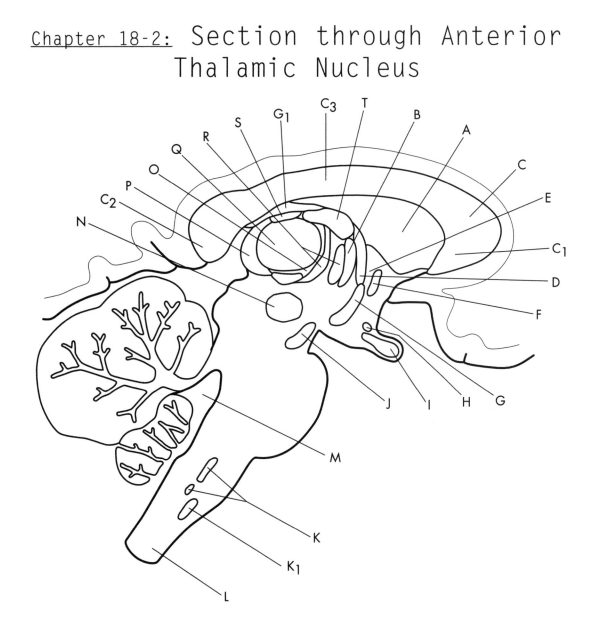

○	Lateral ventricle	A	○	Anterior commissure	F	○	Fourth ventricle	M

○	Lateral ventricle	A
○	Ventral anterior nucleus	B
○	Genu of corpus callosum	C
○	Rostrum of corpus callosum	C₁
○	Splenium of corpus callosum	C₂
○	Body of corpus callosum	C₃
○	Stria medullaris	D
○	Stria terminalis	E

○	Anterior commissure	F
○	Fornix	G
○	Body of fornix	G₁
○	Supraoptic nucleus	H
○	Optic chiasm	I
○	Substantia nigra	J
○	Inferior olivary nucleus (dorsal accessory)	K
○	Inferior olivary nucleus (principal)	K₁
○	Pyramid	L

○	Fourth ventricle	M
○	Red nucleus	N
○	Internal medullary lamina	O
○	Pulvinar	P
○	Dorsal medial nucleus	Q
○	Ventral lateral nucleus	R
○	Lateral dorsal nucleus	S
○	Anterior thalamic nucleus	T

Chapter 18-3: Section through Dentate Nucleus

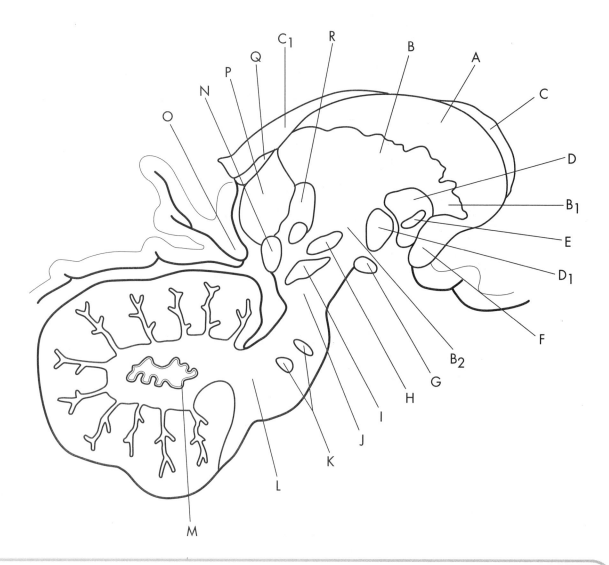

○ Caudate nucleus	A	○ Globus pallidus (external segment)	D	○ Pontine nuclei	K
○ Genu of internal capsule	B	○ Globus pallidus (internal segment)	D_1	○ Middle cerebellar peduncle	L
○ Anterior limb of internal capsule	B_1	○ Anterior commissure	E	○ Dentate nucleus	M
○ Posterior limb of internal capsule	B_2	○ Putamen	F	○ Medial geniculate nucleus	N
○ Anterior horn of lateral ventricle	C	○ Optic tract	G	○ Cingulate gyrus	O
		○ Subthalamic nucleus	H	○ Pulvinar	P
○ Body of lateral ventricle	C_1	○ Substantia nigra	I	○ Crus of fornix	Q
		○ Basis pedunculi	J	○ Ventral posterior lateral nucleus	R

Chapter 18-4: Section through Hippocampal Formation

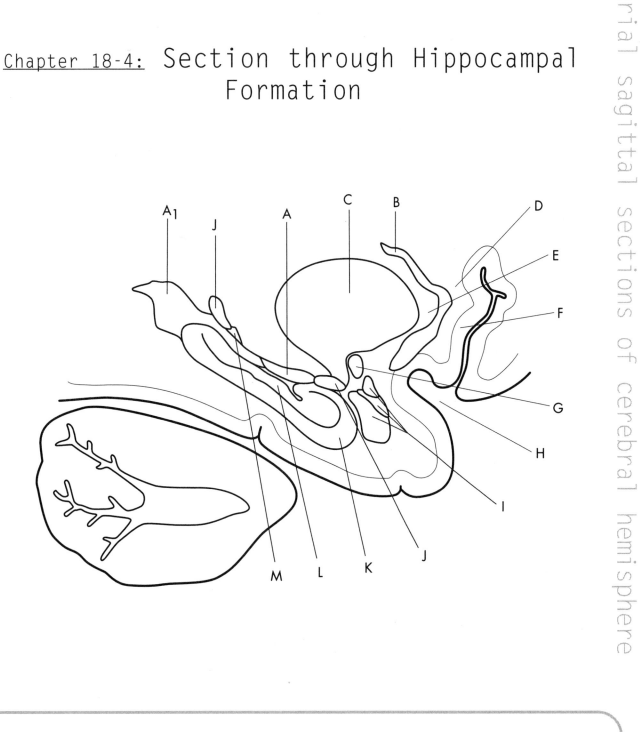

○	Inferior horn of lateral ventricle	A	○ Extreme capsule	D	○ Amygdaloid complex	I
○	Posterior horn of lateral ventricle	A₁	○ External capsule	E	○ Tail of caudate nucleus	J
○	Claustrum	B	○ Insular cortex	F	○ Hippocampus	K
○	Putamen	C	○ Anterior commissure	G	○ Dentate gyrus	L
			○ Lateral sulcus	H	○ Stria terminalis	M

the human brain atlas

serial horizontal

sections

Following is a series of horizontal sections of the brain. They proceed in sequential order from dorsal to ventral (superior to inferior), each progressive section being ventral to the one before.

Chapter 19-1: Section through the Body of the Lateral Ventricles

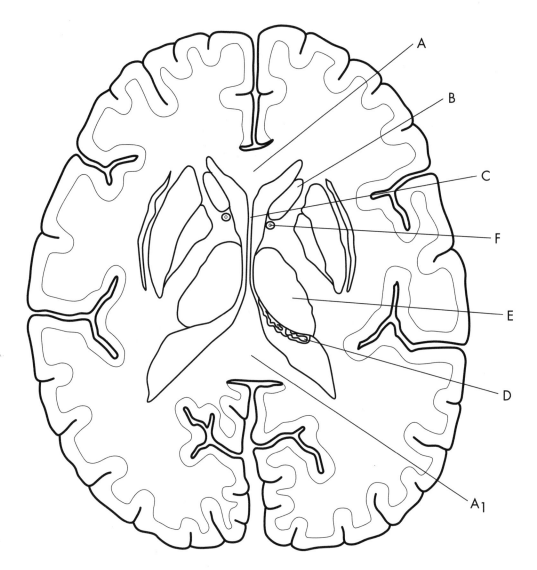

○ Genu of corpus callosum	A	○ Caudate nucleus	B	○ Thalamus	E
○ Splenium of corpus callosum	A₁	○ Septum pellucidum	C	○ Stria terminalis	F
		○ Choroid plexus	D		

Chapter 19-2: Section through Genu of Internal Capsule

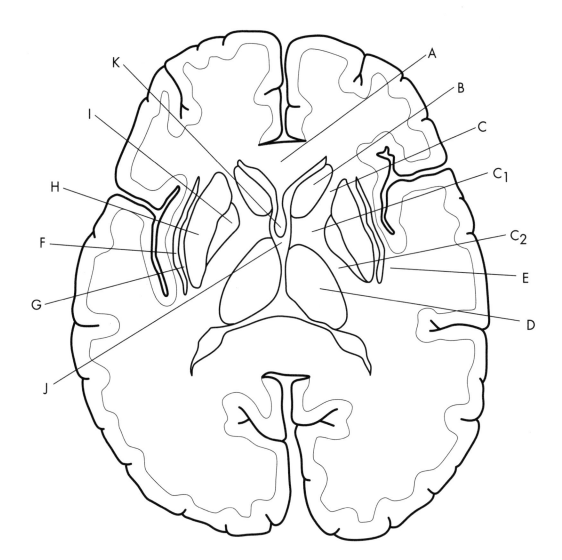

○ Genu of corpus callosum	A	○ Posterior limb of internal capsule	C_2	○ Putamen	H
○ Caudate nucleus	B	○ Thalamus	D	○ Globus pallidus	I
○ Anterior limb of internal capsule	C	○ Extreme capsule	E	○ Interventricular foramen	J
○ Genu of internal capsule	C_1	○ Claustrum	F	○ Column of fornix	K
		○ External capsule	G		

Chapter 19-3: Section through Thalamus

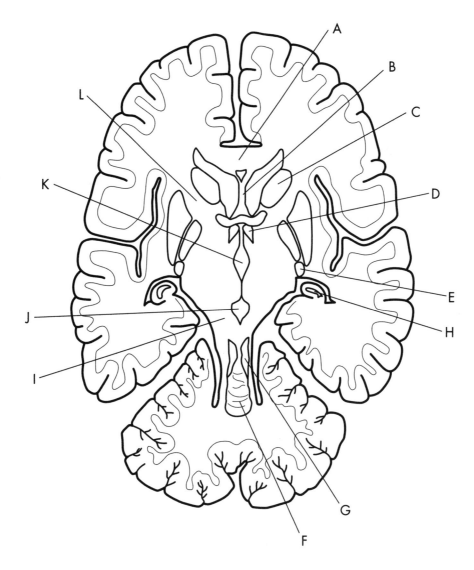

○ Body of corpus callosum   A

○ Septum pellucidum   B

○ Head of caudate nucleus   C

○ Column of fornix   D

○ Anterior commissure   E

○ Vermis of cerebellum   F

○ Fourth ventricle   G

○ Hippocampal formation   H

○ Crus cerebri   I

○ Interpeduncular fossa   J

○ Third ventricle   K

○ Anterior limb of internal capsule   L

Chapter 19-4: Section through Midbrain

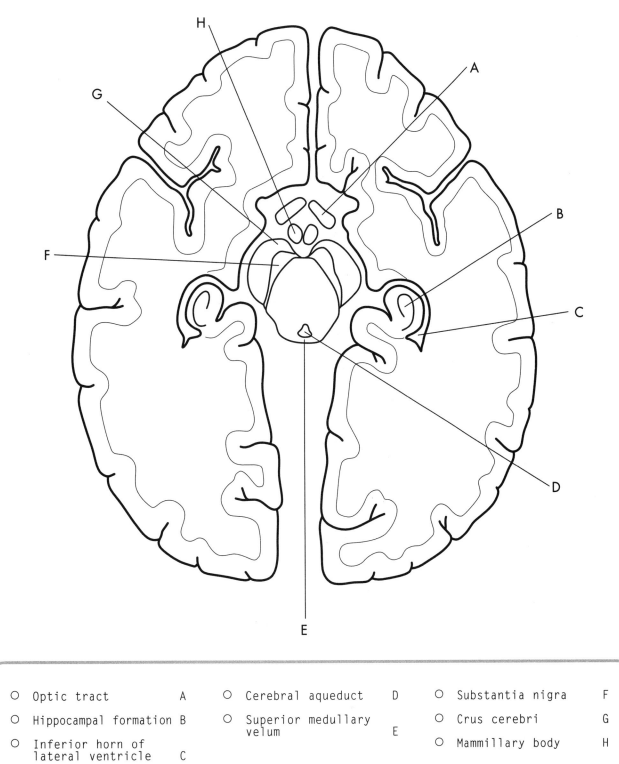

H

G

A

B

F

C

D

E

○	Optic tract	A	○ Cerebral aqueduct	D	○ Substantia nigra		F
○	Hippocampal formation	B	○ Superior medullary velum	E	○ Crus cerebri		G
○	Inferior horn of lateral ventricle	C			○ Mammillary body		H

CHAPTER TWENTY

the human
brain atlas

brain stem topography

Chapter 20-1: Dorsal Surface of Brain Stem (with cerebellum removed)

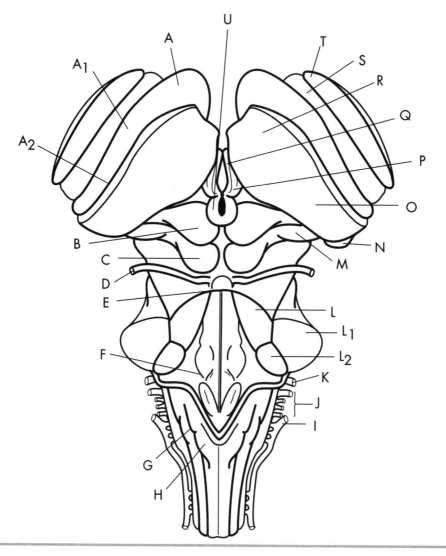

○	Head of caudate nucleus	A	○	Cuneate tubercle	G	○	Medial geniculate body	M
○	Body of caudate nucleus	A₁	○	Gracile tubercle	H	○	Lateral geniculate body	N
○	Tail of caudate nucleus	A₂	○	Spinal accessory nerve (CN XI)	I	○	Pulvinar	O
○	Superior colliculus	B	○	Vagus nerve (CN X)	J	○	Habenula	P
○	Inferior colliculus	C	○	Glossopharyngeal nerve (CN IX)	K	○	Stria medullaris	Q
○	Trochlear nerve (CN IV)	D	○	Superior cerebellar peduncle	L	○	Thalamus	R
○	Superior medullary velum	E	○	Middle cerebellar peduncle	L₁	○	Internal capsule	S
○	Sulcus limitans	F	○	Inferior cerebellar peduncle	L₂	○	Putamen	T
						○	Pineal gland	U

Chapter 20-2: Ventral Surface of Brain Stem

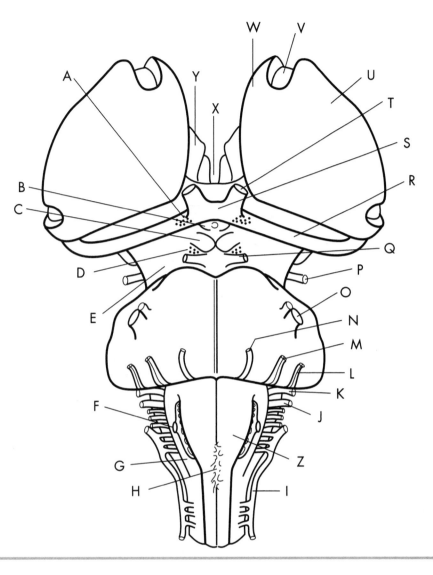

○ Anterior perforated substance	A	○ Vagus nerve (CN X)	J
○ Infundibulum	B	○ Glossopharyngeal nerve (CN IX)	K
○ Mammillary body	C	○ Vestibulocochlear nerve (CN VIII)	L
○ Posterior perforated substance	D	○ Facial nerve (CN VII)	M
○ Basis pedunculi	E	○ Abducens nerve (CN VI)	N
○ Hypoglossal nerve (CN XII)	F	○ Trigeminal nerve (CN V)	O
○ Olive	G	○ Trochlear nerve (CN IV)	P
○ Pyramidal decussation	H	○ Oculomotor nerve (CN III)	Q
○ Spinal accessory nerve (CN XI)	I		

○ Optic tract	R
○ Optic chiasm	S
○ Optic nerve (CN II)	T
○ Putamen	U
○ Internal capsule	V
○ Head of caudate nucleus	W
○ Third ventricle	X
○ Thalamus	Y
○ Pyramid	Z

Chapter 20-3: Lateral View of Brain Stem

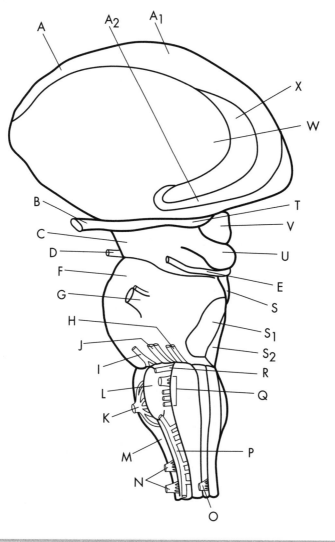

○ Head of caudate nucleus	A	○ Vestibulocochlear nerve (CN VIII)	H	○ Vagus nerve (X)	Q
○ Body of caudate nucleus	A_1	○ Abducens nerve (CN VI)	I	○ Glossopharyngeal nerve (IX)	R
○ Tail of caudate nucleus	A_2	○ Facial nerve (CN VII)	J	○ Superior cerebellar peduncle	S
○ Optic tract (CN II)	B	○ Hypoglossal nerve (CN XII)	K	○ Middle cerebellar peduncle	S_1
○ Basis pedunculi	C	○ Olive	L	○ Inferior cerebellar peduncle	S_2
○ Oculomotor nerve (CN III)	D	○ Pyramid	M	○ Lateral geniculate body	T
○ Trochlear nerve (CN IV)	E	○ Ventral roots	N	○ Inferior colliculus	U
○ Pons	F	○ Dorsal root	O	○ Superior colliculus	V
○ Trigeminal nerve (CN V)	G	○ Spinal accessory nerve (CN XI)	P	○ Putamen	W
				○ Internal capsule	X

the human spinal cord atlas

transverse sections of the spinal cord

Chapter 21-1: Transverse Section of Cervical Cord

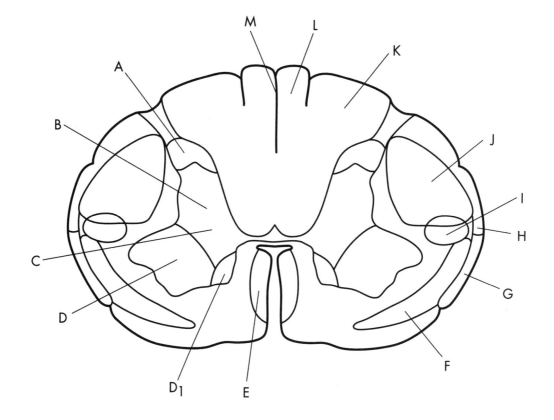

○ Substantia gelatinosa A	○ Anterior cortico- spinal tract E	○ Rubrospinal tract I
○ Dorsal horn B	○ Anterolateral system F	○ Lateral cortico- spinal tract J
○ Intermediate zone C	○ Ventral spinocere- bellar tract G	○ Fasciculus cuneatus K
○ Motor nuclei (lateral) D	○ Dorsal spinocere- bellar tract H	○ Fasciculus gracilus L
○ Motor nuclei (medial) D₁		○ Dorsal median septum M

Chapter 21-2: Transverse Section of Thoracic Cord

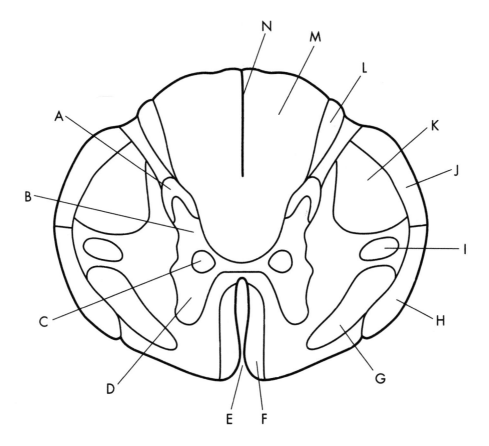

○ Substantia gelatinosa A	○ Anterior cortico-spinal tract F	○ Dorsal spinocere-bellar tract J
○ Dorsal horn B	○ Anterolateral system G	○ Lateral cortico-spinal tract K
○ Clarke's nucleus C	○ Ventral spinocere-bellar tract H	○ Fasciculus cuneatus L
○ Medial motor nuclei D	○ Rubrospinal tract I	○ Fasciculus gracilus M
○ Ventral median fissure E		○ Dorsal median septum N

Chapter 21-3: Transverse Section of Lumbar Cord

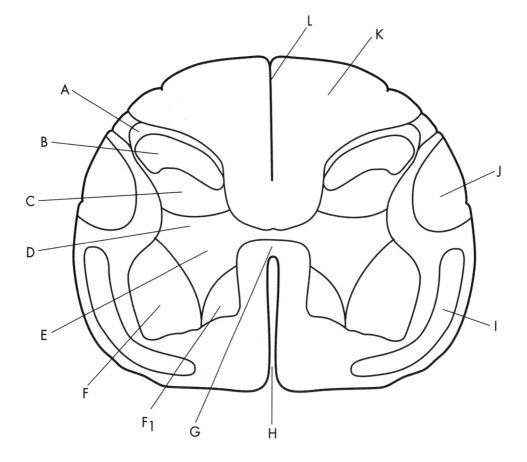

○ Marginal zone	A	○ Motor nuclei (lateral)	F	○ Anterolateral system	I
○ Substantia gelatinosa	B	○ Motor nuclei (medial)	F₁	○ Lateral cortico-spinal tract	J
○ Nucleus proprius	C	○ Ventral commissure	G	○ Fasciculus gracilus	K
○ Dorsal horn	D	○ Ventral median fissure	H	○ Dorsal median septum	L
○ Intermediate zone	E				

Chapter 21-4: Transverse Section of Sacral Cord

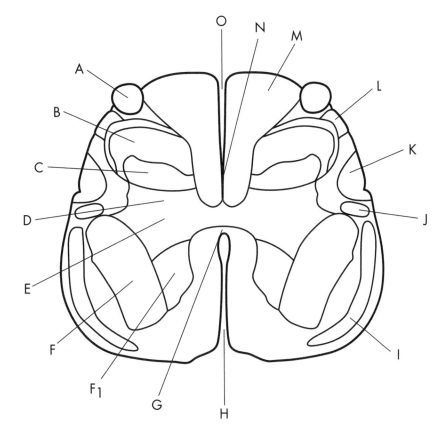

○	Dorsal root	A	○	Motor nuclei (medial)	F_1	○	Lateral cortico-spinal tract	K
○	Substantia gelatinosa	B	○	Ventral commissure	G	○	Zone of Lissauer	L
○	Nucleus proprius	C	○	Ventral median fissure	H	○	Fasciculus gracilus	M
○	Dorsal horn	D	○	Anterolateral system	I	○	Dorsal median septum	N
○	Intermediate zone	E	○	Rubrospinal tract	J	○	Dorsal median sulcus	O
○	Motor nuclei (lateral)	F						

CHAPTER TWENTY-TWO

answer key to self-assessments

CHAPTER 1: THE DEVELOPING CENTRAL
NERVOUS SYSTEM
    1. I
    2. L
    3. J
    4. M
    5. N

CHAPTER 2: THE MENINGES
    1. G
    2. A
    3. D
    4. B
    5. E

CHAPTER 3: THE CEREBRAL
HEMISPHERES
    1. L
    2. E
    3. K
    4. I
    5. F

CHAPTER 4: THE CRANIAL NERVES
    1. C
    2. G
    3. B
    4. H
    5. E

CHAPTER 5: THE VENTRICULAR SYSTEM
AND CEREBROSPINAL FLUID
    1. G
    2. E
    3. J
    4. C
    5. D

CHAPTER 6: THE LIMBIC SYSTEM
    1. C
    2. E
    3. J
    4. B
    5. E

CHAPTER 7: THE THALAMIC COMPLEX
    1. D
    2. H
    3. K
    4. J
    5. B

CHAPTER 8: THE BASAL GANGLIA
    1. C
    2. K
    3. L
    4. M
    5. H

CHAPTER 9: THE BRAIN STEM
1. A
2. A
3. K
4. I
5. G

CHAPTER 10: THE CEREBELLUM
1. C
2. I
3. G
4. J
5. D

CHAPTER 11: THE CEREBROVASCULAR
SYSTEM
1. C
2. F
3. A
4. K
5. I

CHAPTER TWENTY-THREE

index

About the Author

Dr. Kapil Gupta completed a postdoctoral research fellowship in the neurosciences at the University of Connecticut Health Center, an adjunct professorship at the University of Hartford, and part of his medical training at the Baptist Hospital/Bowman Gray School of Medicine. He is the author of two other medical books, *Concepts in Physiology* (Parthenon, 1996), and *Concepts in Microbiology, Immunology and Infectious Disease* (Parthenon, 1997).

FIND US...

International

Hong Kong
4/F Sun Hung Kai Centre
30 Harbour Road, Wan Chai,
Hong Kong
Tel: (011)85-2-517-3016

Japan
Fuji Buibing 40, 15-14
Sakuragaokacho, Shibuya Ku,
Tokyo150, Japan
Tel: (011)81-3-3463-1343

Korea
Tae Young Bldg, 944-24,
Daechi- Dong, Kangnam-Ku
The Princeton Review- ANC
Seoul, Korea 135-280,
South Korea
Tel: (011)82-2-554-7763

Mexico City
PR Mex S De RL De Cv
Guanajuato 228 Col. Roma
06700 Mexico D.F., Mexico
Tel: 525-564-9468

Montreal
666 Sherbrooke St.
West, Suite 202
Montreal, QC H3A 1E7 Canada
Tel: (514) 499-0870

Pakistan
1 Bawa Park - 90 Upper Mall
Lahore, Pakistan
Tel: (011)92-42-571-2315

Spain
Pza. Castilla, 3 - 5º A, 28046
Madrid, Spain
Tel: (011)341-323-4212

Taiwan
155 Chung Hsiao East Road
Section 4 - 4th Floor,
Taipei R.O.C., Taiwan
Tel: (02)751-1243

Thailand
Building One, 99 Wireless Road
Bangkok, Thailand 10330
Tel: (662) 256-7080

Toronto
1240 Bay Street, Suite 300
Toronto M5R 2A7 Canada
Tel: (800) 495-7737
Tel: (716) 839-4391

Vancouver
4212 University Way NE,
Suite 204
Seattle, WA 98105
Tel: (206) 548-1100

National (U.S.)

We have over 60 offices around the U.S. and run courses in over 400 sites. For the courses and locations nearest you call **1 (800) 2/Review** and you will be routed to the nearest office.

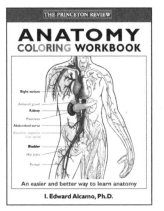